MW01067705

Street Rider's Guide

Project Team
Editor: Andrew DePrisco
Copy Editor: Joann Woy
Design: Mary Ann Kahn
Indexer: Elizabeth Walker

i-5 PUBLISHING, LLC™
Chief Executive Officer: Mark Harris
Chief Financial Officer: Nicole Fabian
Vice President, Chief Content Officer: June Kikuchi
General Manager, i5 Press: Christopher Reggio
Editorial Director, i5 Press: Andrew DePrisco
Art Director, i5 Press: Mary Ann Kahn
Digital General Manager: Melissa Kauffman
Production Director: Laurie Panaggio
Production Manager: Jessica Jaensch
Marketing Director: Lisa MacDonald

Photos: Stephen Mcsweeny/Shutterstock: front cover; Joyce Vincent/
Shutterstock: back cover; iurii/Shutterstock: 1; Bartlomiej Magierowski/
Shutterstock: 5; Dudarev Mikhail/Shutterstock: 13;
all other photos by David L. Hough.

Copyright © 2014 by i-5 Publishing, LLC™

All rights reserved. No part of this book may be reproduced, stored in a retrieval
system, or transmitted in any form or by any means, electronic, mechanical,
photocopying, recording, or otherwise, without the prior written permission of
i5 Press™, except for the inclusion of brief quotations in an acknowledged review.

Library of Congress Cataloging-in-Publication Data
Hough, David L., 1937- author.
  Street rider's guide : street strategies for motorcyclists / by David L. Hough.
    pages cm
  ISBN 978-1-62008-132-7 (alk. paper)
1. Motorcycling--Safety measures. 2. Motorcycling accidents--Prevention. I.
Title. II. Title: Street rider's guide : street strategies for motorcyclists.
  TL440.5.H67225 2014
  629.28'475--dc23
                        2014015346

This book has been published with the intent to provide accurate and authoritative
information in regard to the subject matter within. While every precaution has
been taken in the preparation of this book, the author and publisher expressly
disclaim any responsibility for any errors, omissions, or adverse effects arising
from the use or application of the information contained herein.

i-5 Publishing, LLC™
3 Burroughs, Irvine, CA 92618
www.facebook.com/i5press
www.i5publishing.com

Printed and bound in China
14 15 16 17   1 3 5 7 9 8 6 4 2

Contents

Foreword

Riding a motorcycle skillfully has been compared with the difficulty of piloting a helicopter; there are so many unique controls to master. For instance, braking typically requires the rider to use both a hand lever and a foot pedal, rather than simply stepping on a brake pedal as in a car. And to make matters more complicated, a motorcycle, with its relatively tiny tire contact patches, can transfer so much weight forward under hard braking that properly balancing the applied front and rear brake pressures can be very difficult under the best of circumstances, and can test the skills of the most experienced riders on slippery surfaces. Oh, and rolling on throttle and squeezing the front brake will often need to be combined smoothly when downshifting, another trick of manual dexterity and careful judgment to master.

The same goes for acceleration. As the average motorcycle has the power-to-weight ratio of a race car, but without the traction of four wide wheels, it's also easy to overpower the rear wheel, causing a variety of unplanned events. With a manual clutch, taking off from a stop demands a balance of engine power and clutch slip to master smoothly. Additionally, starting off from a hill will require balancing the bike at a standstill with one foot while simultaneously engaging the rear brake—again a unique combination of skills—and both are a big part of why manual transmissions have nearly disappeared from automobiles.

With all that, the most difficult part of motorcycling to master is steering, or rather countersteering, the uniquely counterintuitive method by which a motorcycle is most efficiently directed through corners. The number of riders that never properly master this technique is probably very large, although it has never been measured to my knowledge. But the failure to negotiate a corner is given as the cause for a high percentage of motorcycle crashes.

Given this level of difficulty, those who do master these control skills to the degree that they can all be done in combination without conscious effort will often find motorcycling the most satisfying experience of their lives. Some even feel it has a mystical or spiritual aspect, as it seems to magically integrate the body and mind into a state of flowing movement.

However, even at this level of mastery, a rider is not yet safe on the road. Even proper riding gear is no insurance against injury in a collision between a motorcyclist and heavy steel vehicles or hard stationary objects. Sharing the road with cars and trucks, a motorcycle is fragile and hard to see, even when drivers are not distracted or otherwise impaired. And conspicuity, the art of making oneself highly visible to other road users, is not enough, either.

The final key to safety is an encyclopedic knowledge of potential road hazards and a full-time situational awareness of how common traffic situations can harbor hidden traps for a motorcyclist. This is the gift that David Hough's latest book is meant to deliver— brief insights into the most common safety hazards and how to avoid them, bite-sized and easy to digest.

As the Editor-in-Chief of *Motorcycle Consumer News* for almost 15 years, America's only 100% subscriber-supported, advertising-free, nationwide monthly motorcycle magazine, the opportunity to communicate with so many committed enthusiasts has been my greatest enjoyment. And when I'd get a letter that shared how one of David's "Proficient Motorcycling" or "Street Strategies" columns had literally saved a reader's life that day, nothing could be more gratifying.

Take these stories to heart and re-read them occasionally. Keep them fresh, in the forefront of your riding decisions, and while you may never be inspired to write a note of thanks for their lessons, I can't imagine that you won't be a better, safer rider for having read this book.

Cheers,
Dave Searle,
Editor-in-Chief, *Motorcycle Consumer News*

Introduction

Your Road to a Million Crash-free Miles

I've spent much of my adult life trying to help street riders manage the risks of motorcycling. It doesn't take very long riding in traffic to understand that survival on a motorcycle is going to require a big bag of riding skills. With more than a million miles of riding in North America and on other continents over the past five decades, I've experienced a lot of different conditions and hazards that have caused serious motorcycle crashes. And I've seen many more that I recognize could cause a crash to an inattentive rider. When possible, I'll stop and take a photo of a hazard so that I can better illustrate the problem. Based on my riding experiences, I've generated hundreds of safety columns for various motorcycle magazines and written several books, most notably *Proficient Motorcycling*. Since *Street Rider's Guide* is intended to help you survive the ride, I want to introduce it with an explanation. It's going to be a bit of a bumpy ride, so hang with me here. Take a break if you need to and then come back.

If you took a basic rider training course, you may have thought that you got a decent introduction to motorcycling, but it's a fantasy to believe that anyone can learn how to ride a bike and survive traffic and surface hazards in two short days. Lots of new riders get their licenses after just one weekend of riding around a parking lot on a training bike. It should be no surprise that lots of new riders have nasty crashes out on public roads.

The first lesson about motorcycling is that it's a lot more dangerous than you might have realized. According to the Centers for Disease Control and Prevention, between 2001 and 2008 in the United States, more than 1.2 million motorcyclists were treated in hospitals for serious injuries, and more than 34,000 died. In the same time frame, crash-related deaths involving cars and light trucks dropped to an all-time low. Motorcycles are only about 4 percent of vehicles on the road, but we rack up about 30 percent of all motor vehicle fatalities.

So, why hasn't rider training had an effect on bringing down the fatality and injury numbers? Rider training was set up in the early 1980s to help new motorcyclists get a quick introduction to the sport. Training seems like a commonsense way to make motorcycling safer, and it did work until around 1997. But, since then, training has morphed from learning to ride a bike skillfully into an easy way to get a motorcycle license. The focus in rider training today is on getting more riders licensed as quickly and as easily as possible. The result of hundreds of thousands of people getting trained and licensed every year is that fatalities have risen to frighteningly high levels, and the fatality rate for motorcyclists is much higher than the rate for other motor vehicle operators.

If you're an average motorcyclist, you are right around 30 times more likely to die when you are riding a motorcycle than when you are driving a car. That's not 30 *percent* higher, that's 30 *times* more dangerous!

That's the dark side of rider training in the United States. Training introduces lots of people to motorcycling, including too many motorcyclist "wannabes" who just aren't motivated to absorb what they need to survive. It's very hard for instructors and rider coaches to accept the results. When you are putting your heart and soul into rider training, it's heartbreaking to come to the awareness that you might be hurting more than you're helping.

We call this field "motorcycle safety," but we should really call it "motorcycle danger." What I try to do is counsel riders to reduce their personal dangers as much as possible. And I know that, with serious attention, it's possible to manage the dangers very well. One of my BMW friends, Voni Glaves, has ridden more than a million miles—without a single crash. I wish I could say the same. Most of us experience one or more injurious crashes during our riding career.

If you're not really serious about motorcycling, consider giving it up. I'm not joking about this. Motorcycling requires full and complete attention. If you're not willing to commit to lifelong study and practice, maybe some other activity would be just as much fun without all the danger. I know, you've seen lots of people riding motorcycles who don't appear to be very concerned about the danger. But then, there are lots of ex-motorcyclists limping around with permanent injuries, not to mention the many who are no longer with us.

If you think you have the right attitude to become a proficient motorcyclist, it's going to be hard work from here on out. You need to continually practice control skills until you can put the bike exactly where you want it to go without any wasted time or thought. Then you must learn how to spot trouble developing so you can get out of the way.

Let's follow a fictitious rider we'll call "Biker Bob." Biker Bob may be fictitious, but he exhibits a lot of traits shared by many real-life riders. Bob started riding a couple of years ago, but hasn't really done anything to improve his skills or knowledge. He just goes riding and assumes that he'll eventually figure it out. One day, Bob rounds a blind corner at 40 mph and is shocked to realize that the pavement is tightening up into a decreasing radius. Bob tries to lean the bike further but just can't stay with the pavement. The bike sails off the road and smacks into a big rock. While Bob is healing and his bike is being repaired, he decides he should take a track course to jack up his cornering skills.

Back on the road again after the track school, Bob marvels at how much easier it is to corner once you master a few skills such as countersteering, following "bike" cornering lines, and sneaking on the throttle during the turn-in. Six months later, Bob is zipping smartly around a blind turn at 60 mph and is startled to see a truck on its side, blocking both lanes. Before Bob can get the bike slowed, he crashes into the truck. What went wrong here? Why didn't increased cornering skill translate into avoiding the second crash?

The answer is that Bob's crashes were mostly a result of poor mental skills, not inadequate control skills. Training Bob to corner faster helped him to have more fun, but his basic problem was poor situational awareness. He just didn't know how to look ahead, how to think about what's not yet in view, or how to link speed to sight distance.

It's essential that a motorcyclist learn the physical skills to control such things as balancing, turning, shifting, and braking. There are more than a few riders around who demonstrate their embarrassing lack of skill by dragging their boots on the pavement or paddle walking the bike around in a U-turn in a desperate attempt to keep the bike from falling. I've seen lots of riders banging down repeatedly on the shift lever because they don't know how to shift smoothly and quietly. Lots of riders follow a "car" line through corners, wasting traction. But poor control skills don't necessarily result in more frequent crashes, especially those that are a result of poor situational awareness. The important message is that you need to figure out how to control the situation as well as the bike.

One big part of controlling the situation is to learn how to look. You need to get your eyes up and reaching out well ahead of the bike, like a fly fisherman casting a line way out into the river and reeling it back in. For a motorcyclist, it's not simply a matter of casting focus out and back, but of scrutinizing the situation for specific hazards, such as loose gravel, an oncoming car that could turn left across your path, or a bicyclist who might cause a driver to swerve across the centerline. The farther ahead you can spot a problem, the more time you have to deal with it. There is no point in looking down at the ground a few feet in front of the bike because that's already history. No one can react instantly. When you're riding along at 60 mph, you're covering 88 feet per second. It takes a second or so to react to what you see, so there's really nothing you can do about the next 88 feet. Successful riders learn to scrutinize the situation way ahead of the bike.

It's not just a matter of a hazard being in front of the bike, but anything around you that could cause you harm. That includes vehicles changing lanes or coming up behind you. The story goes that a motorcyclist was riding home from work and stopped for a red light. A car driver was going the same way, several seconds behind the motorcyclist. The car driver failed to notice the red light or the stopped motorcycle and smashed into the bike without slowing. The motorcyclist died. The woman driving the car was found to have been painting her nails while driving. The lesson here is that, even if you are obeying the laws and not even moving, you can't afford to turn off your "mental radar."

Likewise, you need to comprehend trouble spots even when you can't see another vehicle intruding.

For example, alleyways are almost as dangerous as intersections and more likely to result in fatal collisions. You need to be motivated to think about what might happen if a car zooms out of a narrow alley into your path. Maybe it would help to ease on a little front brake to slow down or to move over to the left side of your lane. Nine times out of ten, there won't be a car emerging from an alley. But if a car does appear, you'll be ready.

The point here is that it's not enough to be on high alert waiting for something bad to happen and then reacting to the emergency. You need to use your brainpower to predict what *might* happen, so that you can position yourself to avoid possible hazards, whether it's a car behind you zooming out of a parking lot, a diesel oil spill, or a missing manhole cover.

I've offered a number of "unbelievable" scenarios at different seminars and training courses over the years, and none of them ever turned out to be as fictional as I had imagined. A few years ago, I was giving a presentation at a big motorcycle event in Minneapolis. My topic was deciding on emergency actions to avoid hazards. *"Here you are, riding down the freeway near Minneapolis, when suddenly you spot an elephant escaped from the zoo and lumbering across the highway. What would you do? Brake? Swerve? Accelerate? Open a bag of peanuts?"*

I thought I was offering a ridiculous situation that might stimulate some dialogue about the different evasive tactics we might use, with a little humor thrown in to entertain the audience. After the seminar, a rider came up to talk with me. "Dave, you're not going to believe this, but last year an elephant did escape from the zoo and tried to cross the freeway."

I eventually learned that there is such a wide array of hazards lurking out there that you must keep your mental radar looking for anything. I can assure you that there is no limit to the hazards you will find out in motorcycle land once you start looking and thinking. Whatever the situation, you must figure out what's happening and avoid getting caught up in the problem.

To help you on your journey toward getting really observant about the riding situation, I've assembled some common crash scenarios into this handbook. Don't feel that you have to read this in any specific order. Take it along with you on your rides, and pop it open to any page while you're taking a break. You'll probably encounter some of these dangers regularly, but don't be surprised when one of the less likely scenarios happens right in front of you. And you can chuckle to yourself, "Dave, you're not going to believe this, but…"

Remembering some of these strategies might just save you from a nasty crash. I hope that thinking about the scenarios in this handbook will help you on your quest to spot hazards for yourself. Maybe you can top a million crash-free miles!

David L. Hough

Alien Asphalt

The best clue about surface hazards is a change in color or texture.

You're out for a ride with some buddies and, at the moment, you're leading the group. The weather has been sunny and warm, and you're pleased that there's almost no traffic on the back roads you're following. You see what appears to be new paving ahead, but there aren't any orange construction signs warning you of a serious hazard. Something about the situation spooks you a bit, but you don't want to be seen as overly cautious, so you maintain speed.

But just as your front tire rolls onto the darker surface, steering gets funny and the bike starts plowing from side to side. You realize the new asphalt is very soft, allowing your tires to sink in. You roll off the throttle and stab at the rear brake pedal to warn the riders behind you, but it's too late. Your front tire digs into the berm of soft asphalt at the center of the lane, and the bike veers toward the ditch. You barely manage to stop in the deep gravel at the side of the new paving without dropping the bike. The next rider isn't so lucky. His bike wiggles around and then muddles into the gravel berm and crashes on its side. The next rider in line attempts to brake quickly enough to stop short of the soft pavement but is rear-ended and knocked down. It's a disaster.

Road maintenance doesn't always work out as planned. Sometimes the asphalt mix comes out very soft or oily and doesn't bond together well enough to roll down firm and smooth. In this situation, the asphalt might eventually pack down under the weight of passing vehicles, but at the moment, it's like soft gravel coated with slippery black oil. If you had looked a bit more carefully, you might have noticed the loose gravel pushed to the sides of the wheel tracks, hinting that perhaps the surface is not as firm as it may appear. You might want to blame the road crew for leaving such a mess, but a big part of your job is to maintain your awareness of the situation and not be surprised by surface hazards.

You know what the surface is like under your tires at the moment because you can feel it. When you see a change in the color or texture of the surface ahead, be suspicious and reduce your speed until you can determine the feel and makeup of the new surface.

Alley Acumen

Alleys are intersections, too.

You're riding home from the hardware store with some fasteners you need to complete a project. You know about the danger of intersections, where other drivers often make sudden turns. You just passed through a busy intersection without incident, so you're mentally relaxing until you get to the next intersection and mulling over your purchase of the 10 mm stainless steel bolts, hoping they are the right length.

Just as the car ahead of you passes an alley, an SUV suddenly begins to pull out. You're startled, but manage to swerve left and avoid a crash. Now you're shaking from the near collision, wondering what you might have done better to avoid the scare.

When riding in traffic, you know that intersections are potentially dangerous, but it's important to recognize that alleys, driveways, streetside businesses, and parking lots also create intersections with the potential for collisions. Alley collisions are typically more likely to be fatal, perhaps because we just don't appreciate the danger there.

Motorcycling is a full-time job, and allowing yourself to be distracted by other thoughts in hazardous locations puts you at additional risk. Surviving the street requires that you maintain your awareness of everything that's happening around you, which includes not only vehicles you can see but your prediction of vehicles you can't see yet, based on the situation.

When you are approaching any intersection where you can see or predict a vehicle on a cross street, including vehicles in alleys, be prepared to take action to avoid a collision. You can change speed to increase separation, but it's usually better to slow down than to speed up. Accelerating increases forward energy, which makes it more difficult to pull off a quick stop or swerve if that becomes necessary.

You could also move farther away from the path of vehicles that potentially could collide with you. For instance, approaching an alley or side street on your right, move to the left side of your lane or even change to the left lane on a multilane street. Establishing eye contact with the other driver doesn't guarantee that he or she won't pull out, but if you can't see the other driver, you *know* he or she can't see you. If you suspect that the other vehicle might pull out, it is smart to brake early to make space, to avoid having to attempt a quick avoidance maneuver in the last couple of seconds.

Arrow Slides

Some of those arrows on the surface can be as slick as ice.

You're on a trip to a different state to visit a friend, and today you're trying to navigate through a confusing neighborhood to find the correct side street. It's not raining at the moment, but the streets are damp. There are some white arrows on the surface, and you momentarily panic that you might be in the wrong lane to go straight. But now you realize the arrows allow you to go straight, so you ignore them. When the light turns green, you attempt to accelerate, but when your rear tire rolls onto the last arrow, it suddenly steps sideways. You're barely able to keep the bike under control and avoid sideswiping the car on your left, but the close call really got your attention, and you now realize those white arrows are very slick.

Different states and different road maintenance departments use different techniques for applying lane markings. Depending on the state and city, some of those white arrows and lines you encounter may be smooth plastic glued to the surface, rather than paint. The smooth plastic is relatively slippery even when dry, but just a little moisture can make them as slippery as ice.

It's always a good tactic to avoid riding over any white surface markings. If you must cross, select a line that carries you over the narrowest portion of the marking.

And when accelerating over a potentially slick marking, it's smart to go easy on the throttle until you're past the hazard. Note that in this city, the crosswalks are marked with parallel lines, allowing you to put your tires between the lines for better traction.

When braking to a stop, temporarily ease off the brakes until your tires are clear of the potentially slick markings. It's also smart to stop short of any surface markings.

Not all states or cities use slick plastic surface markings, but when you're in an unfamiliar area, it's best to assume they are slick until proven otherwise.

Back-end Bashes

Getting through traffic quickly requires that you maintain your situational awareness.

With all the heavy traffic between home and work, you're using the motorcycle for commuting whenever the weather allows. And the more you ride in traffic, the more aggressive you become. Driving the car, it's normal to sit in line waiting for traffic to move. Riding the bike, you can see farther ahead, be more aware of dynamic traffic patterns, and change lanes to take advantage of faster moving traffic.

This morning, someone in the right lane is dawdling, so you're glancing over your left shoulder to see if there's a gap in the left lane. But before you can jump over there, your peripheral vision picks up the brake lights of the truck ahead of you, and you realize the traffic signal has turned red. You squeeze the brake lever, but it's too late. Your front wheel bashes into the back of the truck, and the bike topples over. It's not a high-speed collision, but you're in pain from slamming into the handlebars and then tumbling to the pavement. Worse yet, the collision is your fault.

Riding a bike in commuter traffic requires both proficient skills and good situational awareness. Yes, you can accelerate, brake, and change lanes quickly on a bike, but surviving day after day in heavy traffic requires that you be fully aware of what's happening and not take any unnecessary risks.

It's not wise to follow too closely in stop-and-go traffic or to assume that you have some privilege to weave around other vehicles. In this situation, you should have dropped back a little farther behind the truck ahead and maintained better awareness of the traffic signals. A collision is a wake-up call that your riding is getting too aggressive.

Bike Traps

One more reason to stay out of the center of the lane.

You're on your way to a friend's house. It's not far, and it's a warm day, so you decide to forgo your riding gear. For some reason, everyone seems to be creeping along, and when traffic does start to move, every red light catches the truck ahead of you. You're concerned about your engine overheating and anxious to get moving. You can just see a bit of the signals for the cross street, and, when you see the amber, you prepare to get moving without wasting any time.

But, shortly after the truck begins to move, your front wheel suddenly dives into a slot in the pavement, and the bike comes to a sudden stop, resting on the brake rotors. You're thrown over the handlebars to tumble across the pavement. It's a slow-speed crash, but you're now bleeding and in pain. Apparently, there were some steel plates covering a construction trench, with a narrow gap between the plates. You couldn't see the plates or the gap because the truck was straddling them. It wasn't a hazard for other vehicles, but it was a serious hazard for a motorcycle.

It's important to maintain your awareness of the road surface, as well as monitor traffic and signal lights. It's not clever to pull up close behind another vehicle at a stop because that limits your view of what might be underneath. It's also a good idea to stop in one of the wheel tracks rather than in the middle of the lane because the vehicles ahead can be hiding a surface hazard. It's smarter to favor the left-wheel track of the vehicle ahead and to leave at least one additional bike length to better see hazards such as debris, spilled oil, edge traps, and potholes.

As your hands and arms gradually heal from the "road rash," you'll probably be reminding yourself to wear your protective riding gear on every ride—even for a short trip across town.

Blind Drivers

If you ride in a driver's blind spot, you're risking a collision.

With gas prices on the rise, you're riding the bike to work more and more. While driving your car, you hadn't been as aware of the complexities of traffic, but riding the bike, you're getting a quick education. Riding the bike takes a lot more concentration. There's no such thing as a simple "fender bender" for a motorcyclist.

The weather wasn't bad this morning, but on your commute home it's started to rain, causing you some additional concern. You try to stay out of the center of the lane to avoid the usual grease strip, and you leave lots of following distance behind the car ahead in case traffic begins to slow.

Suddenly, the van on your left swerves into your lane, almost running into you. You're startled by the sudden intrusion, but you manage to swerve over to the right edge of the lane and blow your horn. The van driver doesn't seem to notice and keeps moving right, across your lane and into the next lane. Apparently, he's headed for the next off-ramp. As you're forced into the exit lane, you finally realize what's happening and gingerly reach for the front brake. You barely managed to avoid being sideswiped by the van, and you're furious.

Yes, the van driver was at fault for changing lanes without signaling, but you set yourself up for a collision by riding in the driver's blind spot. Most vehicles have blind spots at the rear quarters, left and right. The driver very likely couldn't see you there, especially with his or her windows and mirrors wet and foggy. In this situation, you should have either pulled up ahead of the van or dropped back farther behind it to give the driver a better chance of noticing you. And when he did pull over, you should have immediately eased on the brakes to separate yourself.

Blind-spot Blunders

Do you think that truck driver in the next lane sees you?

Traffic is bumper to bumper on the freeway this afternoon, so you're riding on full alert. You try to leave enough following distance to avoid running into the car ahead but not so much space as to encourage someone to jump into it. You can't do much to avoid being hit from behind other than to drop back a little more and make sure you dab on the rear brake enough to light up your brake light. It's frustrating and dangerous to be squeezed in between larger vehicles as traffic moves forward a few feet at a time and then stops. Finally, you see what the problem is: the right lane is closed ahead, and all those vehicles must merge into the left lane.

Most of the drivers are politely allowing alternate vehicles to merge, and you plan to do the same. But you're now alongside four trucks, and one of the trucks ahead is already starting to wedge into the left lane. You ease into the left-wheel track to give yourself more space.

Suddenly, you realize the van next to you is moving over. You beep your horn, but the trucker just keeps coming, and you are forced over onto the narrow shoulder to avoid a collision. You accelerate up beside the cab, beeping your horn and waving a fist, and the driver finally sees you, but there is nothing he or she can do now, other than to allow you to merge in front of him or her.

Accept the fact that bikes are small and difficult to see in traffic, and even harder to see in a trucker's mirrors. Riding at the left side of your lane alongside a truck puts you in the trucker's blind spot. The trucker really couldn't see you there. You should never "park" in the blind spot of another vehicle, especially not a truck. Consider moving up alongside the cab. Beep your horn and give the driver a "thumbs up" to announce your presence in a friendly manner. Or, drop back to make room for the truck and flash your headlight to signal the driver you are clear of the truck's back end. The trucker will probably show appreciation by flashing the taillights as a "thank you."

Bucking Bumps

You can handle a little bump, right?

You've cleared away enough home projects to be able to get away for a weekend ride. The weather is perfect, the bike is running great, and you're looking forward to a two-day trip to clear your head. You've ridden this same highway many times, and you know its tricks and turns, so you can relax and enjoy the ride.

A few miles out of town, you're surprised to see dust ahead on the paved highway. You're wondering if there has been an accident. But then you see some construction signs. You slow down to about 40 mph, and when you see a Bump sign you place more of your weight on the footpegs to absorb the probable impact.

But, just as you reach the "bump," you realize it's a trench that has been cut across the road at an angle rather than straight across the lane. To make matters worse, the trench has been filled with deep loose gravel that is now lower than the edge of the pavement. You try to get your front tire bounced up over the far edge, but instead it plows along in the gravel, and the bike crashes on its side. It's not a serious crash, but you're embarrassed because you thought you could handle a little "bump."

A Bump sign indicates a difference in level between two surfaces, even if the bump is at an angle crossing the lane. When you see construction signs, put your brain on full alert and try to figure out the nature of the situation. Until you know what's happening, it would be wise to slow down. When you realized the hard edge was at an angle, you should have steered farther away from the edge and then swerved back toward it at a greater angle, preferably 45 degrees or more.

Bumper Bikes

Getting rear-ended can ruin your day.

Traffic has been heavy today on the freeway, and you're glad to finally be on a surface street headed for home, alongside your riding buddy. You're overheated, fatigued, and frustrated at traffic, and you're looking forward to a hot bath and a cold beer.

You'd prefer to have more space ahead and behind, but other drivers seem to want to tailgate. And, if you drop back far enough for comfort, someone swerves over in front of you. So, you just do the best you can and hope no one does anything stupid. You do cover the brake lever, move over toward the left side of the lane, and make sure you squeeze hard enough to activate your brake light. You realize you're not going to get home on time, and you steal a glance at the clock to see how late you're going to be.

When you look up again, you see the brake lights of the car ahead. You quickly squeeze on the front brake to bring the bike to a stop. But the driver behind you doesn't seem to comprehend what's happening and slams into the back of your buddy's bike, pushing it

ahead into the stopped car. Neither of you are injured, but now you'll have to stick around to deal with the accident and maybe help transport the damaged bike.

Even if you're almost home, don't let your guard down. Moving over to the left side of the lane was smart and covering the brake lever was good, but squandering attention on your late arrival distracted you from the situation. In heavy traffic, you must look several vehicles ahead to monitor traffic and brake early when you know you're going to have to stop, to better warn the driver behind you.

Camber Clashes

Off-camber left-handers require special attention.

You've finally found the time to ride some of those twisty roads you've only read about. The road called the "Dragon" through Deal's Gap in North Carolina has been high on your list, and finally you get the chance to ride it. You're enjoying the twists and turns, but you're constantly amazed at how quickly the pavement changes direction and shape. You have to work hard just keeping the bike within your lane. It's a fun ride, and you gradually increase your pace as you gain confidence.

Just when you thought you had the "Dragon" tamed, you carve into a left-hander and run out of leanover clearance. Your sidestand slides along in a trail of sparks, levering the bike up until the rear tire loses traction. The rear end slides out, and the bike drops into a muddy ditch. You're not seriously injured, thanks to armor in your riding gear. But there is much broken plastic that will need serious repairs before you can continue the trip.

Almost all twisty roads have one or more dangerous corners. If you're not intimately

familiar with a road, it's best to ride very conservatively and follow smart cornering lines. Be aware that left-handers are often more dangerous than right-handers, due to the camber of the pavement.

Entering this corner, you should have observed the right edge of the pavement disappearing; a strong clue it slants off steeply toward the ditch. You should have immediately braked to reduce speed and lean angle, and shifted your weight to the left. Your cornering lines have a direct bearing on whether you crash or continue. Entering this left-hander more from the right would have pointed the bike toward the level pavement near the center of the road.

Countersteering

Steering the handlebars makes it lean.

You just got into motorcycling a couple of months ago. Now that you have a motorcycle license, you're eager to get out and ride, although it's still pretty scary. Sometimes the bike seems to have a mind of its own.

You feel a lot safer on slower state highways than on the freeways. You drop down into a valley and realize there's a very narrow concrete bridge ahead. Luckily, there's not a big truck coming, but it still looks awfully narrow. You can't keep your eyes off that steel guardrail where it wraps around the concrete. You press your right knee against the tank to urge the bike to lean more toward the left, but it doesn't budge. It just keeps heading toward the guardrail. Finally, you panic and jam on the rear brake to get the bike slowed, just before it bangs into the rusty steel. Your leg is scraped between the bike and the rail, but it doesn't feel broken.

As it happens, we subconsciously steer the bike where we are looking. Staring at the guardrail probably caused you to steer toward it. So, rather than staring at the guardrail, you should have focused on the center of your lane a hundred feet beyond the bridge and ignored the guardrail.

It's very important to understand how to make a two-wheeler turn. To turn, first you have to get the bike leaned. After the bike is leaned, you can steer it. The leaning part is called *countersteering* because you momentarily steer opposite or *counter* to the way you want the bike to go. For instance, to steer the bike more toward the left, you lean it to the left by momentarily pressing on the left handlebar grip. Press left to lean left. Press right to lean right. If this is news to you, it would be wise to spend some time practicing countersteering away from traffic, to get it figured out. By the way, your braking technique needs a little work, too.

Deer Drama

Are those deer warning signs realistic? Yes, they are.

You finally managed to attend a motorcycle rally in Eastern Oregon, and now you're heading for the coast, riding through the fertile John Day Valley. It's cool, so you're wearing all your gear. You notice occasional deer warning signs and wonder about reducing speed. But other drivers don't slow, including pickup trucks with Oregon plates. You wonder if they know something you don't. Are those deer signs realistic? The only deer you've seen have been out in the fields. You decide to maintain speed.

Suddenly, there's a flash of brown in the roadside greenery and, instantly, there's a buck leaping over the guardrail directly into your path. You are so startled you don't even roll off the throttle as the bike slams into the deer and cartwheels. You remember a short flight and then the unforgettable crunching impact as you slam into the pavement. When you come to, you struggle to remember what happened and then realize you are lying in the road with several other motorists gathered around to help. The medics have been called. Your trip is over for today—and for the rest of the year—but you're alive, thanks in part to your gear.

Yes, the deer signs are realistic. They are posted when there have been an abnormally high number of deer strikes in that area. Deer don't seem to have any instinctive fear of motor vehicles, and in areas such as this, there are hundreds of deer strikes every month between spring and fall. The locals don't slow down because deer strikes are treated as an unfortunate risk. When a heavier vehicle such as a pickup truck hits a deer, the driver is protected by crumple zones, belts, and airbags. But when a motorcyclist hits a deer, the results can be serious injury.

Yes, it's wise to slow down when you are passing through deer warning zones and to cover the brake lever. At a slower pace, you will have more time to spot a deer and take evasive action. And, if you can't avoid a deer, the impact forces are less at slower speeds. If other drivers (or riders) choose to not slow down, move over and let them by.

Delusive Drivers

A driver can't signal his intentions if he hasn't decided what to do.

You're out for a ride in the country, following a secondary highway that wanders past farms and the occasional family store. There are lots of twists and even right-angle turns, and a few railroad-grade crossings, but everything is well marked. You've ridden this road before and have a pretty good idea of the layout. The weather is warm and dry today, the surface is clean and predictable, and the bike begs to be ridden aggressively. You can't resist. Most of the road is posted 55 mph, but it feels better at 70. You feel comfortable taking the 25-mph corners at 40.

Approaching a left-hander near a country store, you decelerate, ease over to the right edge of the pavement, and prepare to accelerate just as soon as you are over the railroad tracks. The driver ahead appears to be slowing to turn off at the store, and you plan to pass him on the left.

But, rather than continue his turn, the driver suddenly brakes to a stop right over the railroad track. You can't pass on his left because now there's an oncoming SUV. You apply both brakes just short of skidding, but at the speed you're traveling, you're running out of room. You ease over toward the right to avoid a collision with the car, but your front wheel slams into the exposed rail, putting a huge dent in the rim.

It may be fun to ride the backroads at spirited speeds, but you need to slow immediately for situations that are out of your control, such as wild animals, sightseeing trains, or tourists who are lost or unsure. There are at least three vehicles here that could suddenly get in your way.

In this situation you should have reduced speed much sooner and waited for the other drivers to get out of the way before deciding your move. It's important to be in full control of the bike, but it's just as important to be in control of the situation.

Detour Dumping

Sooner or later, you'll find yourself riding off pavement.

You've had a great road trip so far, and it's only another hundred miles from home when you see a big orange construction sign and a line of cars. You don't like riding on gravel, and you're incensed that the highway department would tear up the whole road and expect a motorcyclist to ride through a dusty detour. You don't have a choice here. If you want to get home, the only route is through the construction zone.

Fortunately, the flagger sees you and waves you up to the head of the line. Later, you'll appreciate that following directly behind the pilot car keeps you out of most of the dust and flying stones. When it's time to go, you try to keep up with the pilot car, but the driver sometimes goes faster than you would prefer on the loose gravel and soft sand. At one point, the surface turns to deep gravel, and you slow way down and hold your boots out to help maintain balance. To little avail as your front tire suddenly tucks and down you go. The driver of the pilot car helps you get the bike upright, but you're angry at the highway department and embarrassed at dropping your bike.

When you need to get through a surface hazard such as deep gravel or muddy ruts, it won't help to go too slow or to stick your boots out like skids. Place more of your weight on the footpegs, to help balance, and roll on enough throttle to keep the bike moving.

Sooner or later, all of us will encounter a situation that requires riding off pavement. A good way to prepare yourself for off-pavement riding is to borrow a lightweight dirt bike and get in some saddle time. Many of the "dirt" skills learned on the smaller bike will transfer to your roadburner, giving you more confidence and better control.

Edge Traps

Those raised pavement edges in construction zones can be your downfall.

You're working your way across town when you encounter a construction zone where the crews are grinding away the old pavement in the right lane to prepare for repaving. The rough surface really vibrates the bike and causes the front wheel to dart back and forth. It makes you nervous. The other lane still has the old paving, which appears to be clean and smooth, and you're thinking about moving over. There aren't any cones or signs prohibiting you from changing lanes. Then, for whatever reasons, traffic in the right lane slows down. That's it! You're going to ease over into the left lane to avoid getting stopped by the traffic light.

But as you attempt to ease over onto the old pavement, the front wheel is suddenly redirected by the pavement edge, and it steers along the edge, not over it. Before you can wrestle it back under control the bike slams over onto its left side in a shower of broken plastic. Your decision to wear your riding gear today really paid off. You're injuries are limited to bruises. You're wondering why the bike toppled over so quickly. The pavement edge is only 3 or 4 inches high.

Remember that two-wheelers are balanced by steering the front wheel to position the contact patches beneath the center of mass. When your front tire contacted the raised edge at a narrow angle, it was steered along the edge rather than over it. When you couldn't steer the front wheel, you couldn't keep the bike balanced. Because of the way raised edges trap the front wheel, they are often called "edge traps."

When you need to get the bike up and over a raised edge, steer away and then come back toward the edge at a greater angle, preferably 45 degrees or more. Add a little throttle to help drive the tire up and over, and then straighten out. It's the same way you would bounce up onto a curb.

Fixation Follies

The bike tends to go where you're looking.

You're surprised how fast traffic is moving along on this urban arterial, considering the number of cars on the road. You're not trying to rush, but you aren't dawdling either. You know you should leave more distance behind the vehicle ahead, but leaving too much space encourages other drivers to jump in front of you.

Approaching an intersection, you're watching the light, trying to predict whether it's about to turn red. You cover the front brake in order to do an aggressive stop if needed. But suddenly the car ahead uncovers a nasty piece of debris you hadn't noticed. It's steel, it's got sharp edges, and it's right in your path. You can't take your eyes off it. And, sure enough, WHAM, your front tire hits it. You manage to keep the bike upright, but you can feel the tire going soft as it loses air.

You're the victim of "target fixation," the tendency to steer a vehicle toward an object of attention. You were staring at the steel debris, and that's where you subconsciously pointed the bike.

To avoid debris or other surface hazards, it's important to maintain a sufficient following distance to be able to see what's under the vehicle ahead. It also helps to look over and around vehicles ahead to spot surface hazards. If you can't drop back, at least ride in the wheel tracks of the vehicle ahead. And when you do see something, it's essential to avoid staring at it: instead, look for a path around the problem. For instance, in this situation, you could have focused on the clear pavement to the left of the steel debris and that would have helped steer the bike around it.

Frog Fixation

Beware those old railroad tracks in industrial areas.

You're trying to find a business in an industrial area. Eventually, you realize the business is in an old warehouse on a side street, only accessible through a bumpy alley. Apparently, this location was once the railroad access to the loading docks of warehouses, and the old rails have gradually been abandoned.

You know how easily a slippery steel rail can divert a front wheel and cause a crash, so you're trying to just ease through this mess of rails and connections. You're really nervous about the X-shaped connections, which are made of huge steel castings (called "frogs"). Although you want to avoid the most slippery parts of the rails, you are fascinated with one connection, which has both sharp steel plates and deep holes. You suddenly realize the bike is headed right into the V-shaped hole outlined with steel. Before you can do anything, your front tire drops into the slot and wedges tightly. The bike comes to an immediate stop, and you're pitched off. You're not seriously injured, but you're really shocked at how easily the rail connections brought you down.

Where there are railroad tracks on side streets, there are likely to be lots of connections to allow for multiple sidings. The rails may have very little use or may even have been abandoned, but they remain as serious surface hazards for motorcyclists. Where a wide car tire is more likely to bounce over a rail or hole, a motorcycle tire may be narrow enough to drop in and wedge tight. Your crash is a typical example of *target fixation*—the bike heading for where you are looking. Staring at the frog cued your subconscious to steer the bike toward it.

If possible, avoid such streets entirely. If you must ride there, plan a line that carries your tires over the rails at maximum angle, while avoiding all of the complex plates, holes, and those damn frogs. Most importantly, avoid staring at the hazards. Focus on where you want the bike to go.

Gravel Grovels

Maybe it's time to work on your off-pavement skills.

One of your riding buddies has moved to a new house, and you're on the way to check out his big workshop. As you continue down the residential road, you see some orange signs indicating roadwork. When you get closer, you realize the road ahead has been oiled and graveled. It appears smooth enough, so you continue along at the 25 mph posted speed.

When your tires drop off the asphalt into the gravel, you're surprised to find it so deep. Your front wheel plows back and forth, causing the bike to dart from side to side. Your survival reaction is to stick your legs out and use your boots like skis to help prevent a slideout. But when the bike drifts over toward the center of the road, the front wheel tucks in a deep berm and the bike heads off the road, crashing in the deep grass. Fortunately, there isn't a hidden ditch or rock, so there isn't much damage, and you're not hurt—except for your pride. You right the bike and arrive at your friend's place with bits of grass hanging from the frame. You have to weather a few minutes of good-natured ribbing.

You should always take warning signs seriously, including the recommended speed. Freshly spread gravel will be loose, and it's usually deeper in areas where passing car tires have pushed it aside. So, it's best to keep your tires in the wheel tracks where other vehicles have packed it down. When negotiating any slick or loose surfaces, it's best to load more of your weight onto the footpegs. That places your weight low on the bike and allows you to keep the wheels perpendicular to the surface. Waggling your legs out contributes to instability and risks injury.

If loose gravel makes you nervous, the solution is to spend a day or two riding gravel roads to improve your techniques and confidence. You might prefer to borrow a dirt bike for your initial practice.

Groovy Surprises

A pavement groove can be your downfall if you aren't paying attention.

You're heading for a rally in a neighboring state, riding the freeway to minimize travel time. Traffic has been light, the weather has been pleasant, and the bike is running smoothly. You're looking forward to the rally, where you'll rub elbows with like-minded motorcyclists and perhaps take in a seminar.

You see orange signs ahead warning of highway construction, and you realize that all traffic is being diverted onto one side of the center barrier. You slow to the 45 mph limit and ease over toward the detour lane, as directed by the barrels and cones. There's a patch of temporary asphalt laid to make the transition, and you plan a smooth line over to the detour.

But just as your front wheel reaches the concrete pavement, it darts to the right, instantly leaning the bike left. You press hard on the right grip to get it stabilized, but then the bike jumps to the left, threatening to take out the orange pylons. You press hard on the right grip to wrestle it back under control, and then you're motoring smoothly along the detour, as if nothing happened. You're really shocked at how the seemingly inconsequential joint between the asphalt and the concrete caused such a violent wobble.

Because of the way two-wheelers balance and steer, it only takes a shallow groove or a minor change in surface elevation to redirect the front wheel and upset stability. In this situation, the temporary asphalt had been pounded down an inch or two below the elevation of the concrete, creating a hard edge almost parallel to your direction of travel. It's good that you were paying attention to the surface change, and you were right to press on the grips to get the bike leaned the way you wanted to go. But crossing this "edge trap" would have been less dramatic if you had crossed at a greater angle, say, staying more to the right of the asphalt area and then swerving to the left to cross the joint. The concrete pavement provides adequate traction to get straightened out after the swerve.

Group Rides

Riding in a group is harder than riding by yourself.

You've gradually gotten to know a few riders who seem to enjoy motorcycling much like you do. They all ride the same brand of machine as you do. They are about your age. And based on what they tend to buy at the local dealer, you suspect that they are as interested in safe riding as you are. After a few interesting conversations at the dealership, you've been invited to join the group for a Saturday ride. It won't be a big group, just a dozen or so riders. You're a little nervous about riding in a group, but you're willing to try it.

You arrive for the breakfast meeting a bit late and, by the time you've eaten, you realize that most of the other participants are already in the parking lot having some sort of discussion. You barely get your gear on, and they are starting to depart. You fall in at the tail end and try to figure it out. You've seen biker movies where they rode side by side, and you try that, but the rider alongside shouts something to you and waves you to drop back. Then he keeps watching you in his mirrors and waves for you to speed up. It's frustrating because you don't know what's expected of you.

Riding in a group can be enjoyable once you learn the ropes, but it is more difficult than riding by yourself because you must be aware of what the group is doing as well as watching surrounding traffic and surface hazards. Different groups have different rules, and you need to comply with the ride leader's directions. A good leader of a safe group not only keeps the riders moving at a reasonable pace but holds a meeting prior to departure to explain the rules, the route, and the schedule. You would have learned a lot if you had managed to attend the riders' meeting.

If it's a "formation" ride, that means everyone will ride together in one group, in a specified arrangement. Staggered formation means riders will alternate left-right, maintaining a suggested following distance to keep the group compact. You position yourself according to the riders ahead and are expected to stay in the formation and spacing determined by the ride leader. Although you might have been put off by the other rider's shouting at you, he was only trying to help you figure it out. If you want to participate in future rides, you would be wise to discuss group riding with the group leader or an informed member of the group. On the other hand, if you attempt to participate in a group ride only to discover that leadership is lax and the information lacking, you would be wise to excuse yourself and look for a safer group.

Headwind Harassment

Why is the bike being blown all over the road?

You've been out for a Sunday ride and, on your way home this afternoon, you're encountering stiff headwinds through a gorge. The bike is being pushed around by the wind gusts, and you're having trouble staying in your lane. Not only does the wind hit you head on, but there are also frustrating gusts from left and right. It may be a coincidence, but every time you round a bluff on your right, you get slammed by a strong gust from the right that threatens to push you across the centerline. You swear the wind sees you coming and creates a blast at the most dangerous time just to frustrate you.

Wind isn't really malevolent. It just moves predictably. To reduce your frustration, it helps to understand how moving air reacts to obstructions such as hills. Imagine riding into a direct headwind. Where the wind bumps into a bluff, it will "reflect" off the upwind face. That's why it seems as if the wind is suddenly gusting at you from the side. Actually, in a steady headwind there will be wind reflecting continuously off every bluff. It only seems like a sudden gust because you are riding through the reflected blast.

Keeping the bike in your lane in windy conditions is a matter of countersteering quickly to get the bike leaned *upwind*. That is, when a crosswind hits you from the right, you must press firmly on the right grip to get the bike leaned over to the right. If it's a strong gust, you need to press more aggressively. Then, when you have passed through the crosswind, you need to quickly press on the opposite grip to get the bike rolled upright. You need to be very quick to react to cross gusts.

Riding in gusting winds is very demanding, and the constant aggressive countersteering contributes to fatigue. It's important to wear hearing protection, take frequent rest breaks, and stay hydrated.

Hidden Turners

Stopping for a sign doesn't mean you won't get hit.

You're riding to work along an arterial street. Traffic is light for a morning commute, and the weather is pleasant. You're very aware of intersections and that left-turning vehicles are a major collision hazard for motorcyclists, so you watch oncoming cars carefully for clues that they are not going *straight* through the intersection. You also watch for cars darting from side streets and alleys since you know these motorists cause a high proportion of motorcyclist fatalities.

As you approach an intersection, you don't see any vehicles on the side streets. There is a bus in the left lane waiting to turn. You predict that the bus won't cause you any problems, other than the rear end swinging wide, so you stay just to the right of the left-wheel track. You stop for the Stop sign, then ease out the clutch to continue through the intersection.

But just as you get rolling, a car shoots directly into your path, turning left. You manage to squeeze on the brake just in time to avoid a collision, but it's too close for comfort.

Because the other car was hidden behind the bus, you couldn't see it nor could its driver see you. Like you, the driver made a legal stop, then proceeded to make a left turn, believing perhaps that the way was clear. Of course, he should have turned into the left lane not the right lane. It's wise to understand that intersections are dangerous locations, and it's essential to monitor the other vehicles and predict where they are going to go, so that you can stay out of their way. But you should not plan to proceed through any intersection until you can see that your path is clear. In this situation, your best strategy would have been to ease up alongside the bus until you could make a quick check to the left.

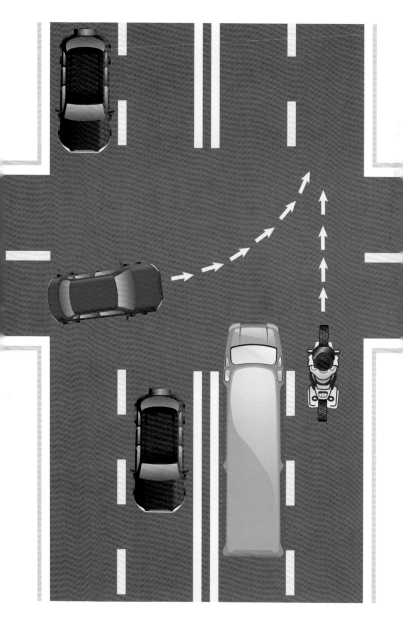

Hiding in Traffic

Just because you can see other vehicles doesn't mean other drivers can see you.

You're headed for the biker café on a Saturday morning. It's been raining for the past couple of days, and you're hoping it lets up in time for the group ride. Your route takes you into the old part of town, where there are lots of alleys and cross streets. You pay special attention to any vehicles that could collide with you. You always ride with your headlight and taillight turned on, and you wear abrasion-resistant riding gear.

The taxi ahead of you stops at an intersection, and you stop close behind. Sitting on the bike you're higher than the roof of the taxi, so you can easily see over the top. When the taxi moves, you follow right along behind, planning to make a right turn.

But just then an oncoming car turns left, right toward you. The driver suddenly sees you and slams on the brakes, but it's too late. The car nails your bike, knocking it sideways onto the curb. You're thrown off, bounce off the hood of the car, and wake up with people staring down at you, asking if you're all right. Soon the medics arrive to strap you onto a gurney and cart you off to the hospital. You keep playing the crash over and over in your mind, wondering what you could have done to avoid it.

Although you might have been able to see the intersection, you were hidden from the view of oncoming drivers by stopping so close behind the taxi. A narrow motorcycle is hard enough to see in traffic. The other driver very likely initiated his turn to pass behind the taxi, not realizing you were there. Of course, he was at fault, but you're the one who was injured. In this situation, dropping back farther behind the taxi and stopping in the left side of the lane would have given the oncoming driver a better chance of seeing you. That would also have given you some maneuvering room.

Although it was a good idea to wear your gear, it should be obvious that riding gear can't do much to prevent injury if you collide with another vehicle. The only way to avoid injury is to maintain your awareness of the situation and not allow yourself to be in a position where you can be hit.

High Siding

Overcooking the rear brake can send you flying.

You've hurried down to the hardware store for a deep socket, and now you're eager to get home with the tool so you can get that oil pressure sender replaced. You're riding briskly on a major arterial with three lanes in both directions. Traffic is moving along at about 50 mph.

You notice a compact car ahead towing a trailer carrying a large yard tractor. It seems to you that the load is way too much for the small car but, of course, that's not your problem. Then the trailer hits some ruts and starts swaying forcefully from side to side. The car and trailer jackknife and roll over, spilling the tractor directly into your lane. You slam on the brakes to avoid hitting it, and your rear tire skids, sliding out to the right. The bike seems about to fall down, so you let up on the brake pedal.

Instantly, the rear of the bike snaps back toward center, and you are pitched off over the right side as the bike flips into two or three violent cartwheels. You're still conscious as you slide to a stop, and you can see cars behind you braking to avoid the mess. Miraculously, you don't get run over, but you know you have some serious injuries from the violent landing.

Braking to avoid a hazard was the proper action, but a better evasive action would have been to slow down sooner to get farther away from the hazardous trailer. But let's focus on your less-than-helpful braking technique. The quickest stop will be with both brakes applied just short of skidding either tire. If the front tire skids, immediately ease up to regain traction and maintain balance. But if the rear tire skids and starts to slide sideways, it's best to keep it skidding. It's possible to bring the bike to a stop with the rear tire skidding sideways. And if you can't keep the bike upright, it's much less violent to let it fall on the low side. In this situation, letting up on the rear brake with the tire sliding out to the side allowed the rear tire to regain traction, precipitating your violent "high side" crash.

Icy Intrusion

Ice in the springtime can really hang you up.

Spring has been a little late this year, and you're itching for a ride. Daytime temperatures have finally warmed up, and the bike is ready to go. With the weather looking good, you arrange a day off work and plan a nice three-day jaunt to a different part of the state. Although you're anxious to get going, you wait until 10 o'clock to set off. You would prefer to avoid frost or ice.

The first day's ride was great, with pleasant temperatures and a hazy blue sky. You really enjoyed getting reacquainted with the bike and exploring some different roads. You have to laugh at yourself for being so paranoid about ice. After a good night's sleep, you set off about 9 o'clock in a different direction that climbs up into the hills. Suddenly, you see a strange reflection in the shadow of a low hill and realize there is solid ice. It looks scary, but you avoid panic and hold the bike steady, just skirting the ice. You feel some unnerving wiggles, but the bike manages to stay upright.

You were right to be concerned about ice. When it's below freezing at night, ice in the shadows can stay frozen long after the air has warmed up. And temperatures will usually be cooler as you gain altitude. The ice you encountered wasn't just frost but solid ice resulting from water overflowing the ditch.

In this situation, your experience helped you to maintain a straight line and avoid any sudden panic reactions. If the bike can maintain traction, it will. It won't help to drag your boots or attempt to change speed. Your course close to the centerline helped avoid most of the ice. Since there was no oncoming traffic, you could have steered over onto the sunny side of the pavement. Most importantly, with the cool nights, you should have predicted ice in the shadows during the morning hours.

Impatient Drivers

Maintain your awareness of everyone around you.

You're on the way home from the big motorcycle rally in Oregon, making time on the freeway. You're not in a hurry, but you always make a point of riding a few mph faster than traffic because you believe that to be safer.

You came up behind a slow-moving "triple" truck that's hogging the passing lane, so you've moved to the right lane to get around. You're being cautious and watching carefully for any clues that the driver might be making a lane change. But, just as you start to accelerate to get past, a fast-moving "road shark" moves up swiftly in the left lane, swerves over to the right lane without signaling, and speeds past the truck. You manage to roll off and swerve to the right to avoid getting sideswiped, but you are startled by the aggressive driving and embarrassed at yourself for failing to see this coming.

If you were annoyed by the slow-moving truck in the left lane, you might have predicted that other drivers would also want to get around it. You might have contributed to the problem by hesitating before accelerating past the truck. The car driver had no way of knowing that you weren't "parked" in the right lane, oblivious to creating a rolling roadblock.

You must constantly maintain your awareness of the entire situation, including other vehicles approaching from the rear in your lane or in adjacent lanes. If you had observed that the car was gaining rapidly on you and the truck, you could have predicted the driver would change lanes to keep out of his way. Alternatively, you could have accelerated sooner to get past the truck without holding up anyone else.

Killer Corner

Every serpentine road has one special corner to challenge your skills.

Heading home from a weekend trip and taking advantage of great weather, you plan to add a few enjoyable miles to your adventure by exploring a curving road that parallels the main highway. You're not familiar with the road, but the pavement looks smooth and dry, and it twists through the trees with a nice rhythm that encourages you to ride briskly. To compensate for the reduced sight distance and possibility of deer, you practice your best cornering skills.

After about a half hour of this awesome road, you determine that the few speed signs are very conservative. You're not too concerned when you see a corner with a suggested 20 mph, but you slow to 45. But, unlike the hundreds of other more predictable corners, this one suddenly tightens up into a decreasing radius, and the surface cambers the wrong way. You push hard on the low grip to tighten your line, but suddenly the bike touches down on the slanting pavement, pushing it even wider. You have no choice but to lift the bike up and brake hard to get your speed down. The bike drifts wide and drops off into the opposite ditch. There's no way you are going to get it back on the road by yourself, even if it still runs.

Next time you head out to explore an unknown road, bear in mind that every serpentine road has at least one corner that's more challenging than the others, perhaps with a decreasing radius, a downhill left-hander, or an uneven surface that eats up ground clearance. Approaching any blind turn, you would be wise to get speed down until you can see through the rest of the curve.

And, if you enter a turn too fast and then need to tighten your line, it is best to maintain a neutral throttle, hang off, and press harder on the low grip to lean the bike to its limits. Focus on where you want the bike to go, and avoid any sudden throttle or brake inputs that would affect traction. Most machines are capable of turning tighter than their owners realize.

Lane Crashing

It's a good idea to look around before you change lanes.

You're heading out for a ride on a Saturday morning, riding the freeway to get out into the country, where you'll pick up one of your favorite twisty roads. You know there's an interchange coming up where drivers will be making last-second lane changes to position for the correct off-ramp, so you've stayed in the left lane. Now, there's a slow-moving van ahead of you. You flash your high beam to signal the driver to get moving or move over, but he doesn't seem to be paying attention. So, you decide to move over to the center lane, flicking on your turn signal as you ease over.

But just as you start to move into the center lane, you're suddenly aware of a car in the right lane heading for the center lane, too. The driver doesn't seem to see you, or doesn't care. You manage to swerve back onto the white line in time to avoid a collision. It's a close call, and you're infuriated at the inconsiderate actions of the other drivers on the road.

Yes, it's inconsiderate to "park" in the passing lane and to change lanes without signaling. But remember that the purpose of turn signals is to let other drivers know what you're going to do, not what you're already doing. You should always signal a minimum of three seconds prior to a lane change.

If there's a collision, the motorcyclist is most likely to win the ride in the ambulance. So, it's up to you to be aware of what's happening and stay out of the way. In this situation, you could have observed the other car moving up and predicted the driver would make a lane change. You could have signaled and then dropped back, so that you would be behind the other car after the lane change.

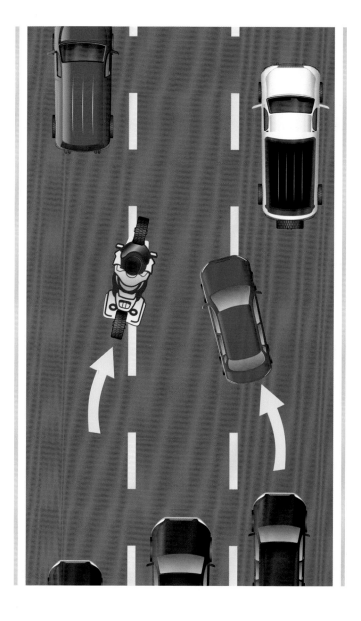

Lane Hoggers

In unfamiliar territory, it's important to think like a local.

You've finally managed to get out to the Northwest to explore the scenery and winding roads. Today, you're riding through some forests, enjoying the greenery and the cool, pitch-scented air. You seem to have the road to yourself, which encourages you to crank up the throttle and enjoy the curves as well as the scenery.

Suddenly, while rounding a right-hander, you see a loaded logging truck coming toward you, and you're shocked to realize the trailer is tracking way over on your side of the pavement. You subconsciously push harder on the right grip to get the bike leaned over more and manage to avoid going under the rear wheels of the trailer. Wisely, you were riding conservatively enough to have some cornering traction in reserve.

You're shocked at how aggressively the trucker came around the corner and his apparent disrespect for a motorcyclist. Actually, the truck driver was very likely not disrespectful but just trying to rush another load of logs to the yard. And, in a tight corner, a truck with a long trailer will take up more than half of the pavement. Like yourself, the truck driver hadn't seen much traffic and probably wasn't expecting to encounter a fast-moving motorcycle on a tight corner.

When you are traveling in unfamiliar territory, it's important to adapt to the local attitudes and hazards. In forested areas out west, logging is common, so you need to be aware of logging trucks, both on the highway and pulling out of forest roads. Local drivers know to give them lots of room.

In this situation, you should have seen or heard the truck coming, realized the trailer might be tracking to the inside of the tight curve, and stayed more to the right side of your lane. That also helps avoid any loose bark or debris that might drop off the logs or any large stones ejected from between the dual tires.

Lane Jumpers

One of your jobs as a motorcyclist is to get out of the way.

You're on a cross-country trip, and this morning you're on a secondary road trying to get around a big city. It's started to rain and traffic is heavy, so you're on full alert for errant vehicles and surface hazards. Suddenly, a car pulls onto the road, right in front of you. The driver must have known you were there, but the guy just ignored you. You're furious, and you beep your horn to show your annoyance, but you ease on the brakes to avoid a rear-ender.

As you ride along in anger, you think about riding up and kicking in the aggressive driver's door with your boot, or worse, but you realize that there really is nothing you can do to defend your road space or command respect. What's more, other drivers might fail to see you at all in the poor conditions. Realize, too, that there are lots of aggressive drivers on the road today with confrontational attitudes, drivers who could literally knock a motorcyclist into a ditch without any remorse. Your only recourse is to get out of the way, get over the insult, and get on down the road.

Let's consider that when you're on a trip, you need not be constrained by the schedules of commuter traffic or the route. You can choose when to get through or around a big city, to avoid the worst traffic, or to take a break to avoid a thunderstorm. Given a choice, avoid riding during the morning and afternoon rush hours. Or, choose a less popular secondary highway farther out in the country.

If you're focusing on the other vehicles around you, you can pretty much tell when another driver intends to change lanes or pull onto the roadway. There really isn't anything you can do to prevent an aggressive driver from elbowing into your lane, and there is no way you can "teach 'em a lesson." The bottom line is, when riding a bike in traffic, you must accept your vulnerability, swallow your indignation, and focus on getting out of the way.

Last Looks

That last look over your shoulder before changing lanes can be a lifesaver.

You're on the freeway heading for work. At the moment, you're being held up by a slow-moving van in the left lane. You also notice that the driver behind you is tailgating. You're not comfortable with the situation, so you decide to change lanes to the right to get around the slow mover. You signal your intention, then start to ease over into the center lane.

But just as you start to move over, you realize the driver who was behind you is also changing lanes and trying to accelerate by you. You manage to tuck back on top of the white line to get out of his way, but his aggressiveness makes you angry.

You were wise to signal your intentions early, but the bottom line is that, whatever happens, you must be prepared to get out of the way. If you're planning a lane change, it's smarter to drop back a little behind a slow mover to allow you to scan the situation with less risk of a rear-ender. But it's essential to take a last look before making your move. You can swivel your head around to look behind, or you can scan in the mirror. If you can't see a wide enough view in the mirror, rocking forward and back in the saddle will allow you to scan more of the situation. That last look before making a move is sometimes called the "lifesaver" for good reason.

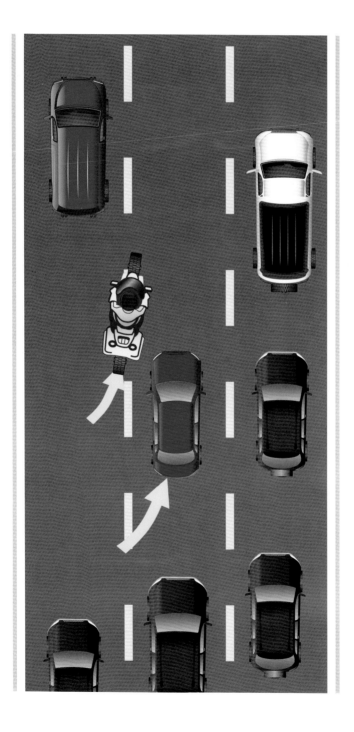

Lethal Left-turners

Your most likely crash in traffic is with a left-turning vehicle.

You're riding along an urban arterial, mulling over a great Saturday ride in the country. The day has been warm and sunny, the bike has been running great, and your favorite circuit of twisty roads was great fun.

Then, just as you enter an intersection on the green light, an oncoming car makes a quick left turn across your path. Without any conscious thought, you make a quick swerve and manage to miss the rear bumper of the car by scant inches. You're instantly furious about a driver being so careless and disrespectful, but you're amazed at your ability to make a quick swerve without having to think about it.

When you are approaching a potentially dangerous situation such as an intersection, it's best to avoid being distracted by thoughts other than what's about to happen. Collisions can occur very quickly, and there's very little time to take evasive action once you realize you're about to crash. The primary way to avoid collisions is to maintain your awareness of the situation into which you are riding.

When faced with a sudden emergency, the human brain takes evasive action based on habits. Therefore, riding somewhat aggressively on that twisty road helped prepare you to *automatically* swerve to avoid the collision. It also helps to practice good braking habits on every ride to develop the muscle memory to brake hard when needed without losing control.

When approaching an intersection where an oncoming driver could possibly attempt a quick left turn, you should realize that about half of the other drivers on the road will fail to observe a motorcycle in traffic, and therefore you should take action early. For instance, you could steer toward the side of your lane opposite the other vehicle, reduce speed, and make evasive maneuvers more likely to succeed.

Intersections are often dangerous locations because of crossing and turning traffic. To help you be better aware of what might happen at an intersection, it helps to study the various collision scenarios. There are actually a few different left-turn situations where another driver could cause a collision, and you should know them all.

Loose Loads

Stay well away from any vehicles with loads that aren't well secured.

You're riding the one and only highway that goes from point A to point B, and you know that traffic is often held up by slower moving drivers or vehicles with strange loads. Today, you've worked your way up through the pack, passing one car at a time. Now, you're directly behind the slow-moving pickup truck that's been holding up traffic.

You'd like to get around the truck as quickly as possible, but something tells you to avoid moving up too close. The truck is carrying what appears to be household junk, including a couch on end, sundry furniture, and giant plastic bags. You can't see any ropes or straps preventing anything from falling out.

Sure enough, the truck goes over a bump and a cabinet comes tumbling out. You're able to brake and then swerve around the cabinet, flashing your brake light three times to warn following drivers. The truck driver is apparently oblivious to losing some of his junk, and he continues on his way.

You were smart to stay well behind this truck. Getting hit by a flying cabinet—or even a plastic bag full of dirty clothing—could knock you off your bike. There are careless drivers around who are apparently willing to risk injuring someone and a fine for an unsecured load. Your best defense is to recognize the problem early and then stay far enough away to avoid being hit by whatever comes bouncing out.

Lousy Lanes

Highways near big cities seem to be in a perpetual state of construction.

You're returning home to the big city from a rally. And the closer you get to home, the worse the roads seem to be. The superslab seems to be in a perpetual state of construction. You changed lanes to get out from behind a truck that was blocking your view and a ladder that wasn't secured very well. But the left lane is narrow, with a hefty concrete barrier just inches away and very uneven paving that bounces the bike around. To make matters worse, some drivers in the right lane are wandering partially into your lane, and it looks like the lanes get even narrower ahead.

You try to stay toward the left side of the lane to avoid getting sideswiped by one of the wandering drivers, but when the concrete divider pinches in, you ease over toward the center of the lane. Suddenly, the bike seems to have a mind of its own. The front wheel darts left and then right. You fight the wobbles, barely managing to keep the bike upright, and finally squeeze over toward the right, braking to position yourself farther from the truck. It's a scary situation.

You were smart to get out from behind a vision-blocking truck and to separate yourself from a potentially loose ladder. But apparently you failed to notice the rutted "edge trap" in the center of your lane, created when the lanes were squeezed in for construction. Two-wheeled motorcycles are especially susceptible to grooves or ruts because they make it more difficult to steer. When you can't steer accurately, it's hard to keep the bike balanced. Your tactic of moving to the right of center and dropping back was good.

In addition to focusing on traffic, you must maintain your awareness of surface hazards, including edge traps like that uneven groove in the center of the left lane. When you must cross a pavement groove or raised edge, swerve across it aggressively, don't try to ease across.

Merging Maniacs

Your mission today is to get out of the way.

Lately, you've been riding the bike to work, not only to save gas but also to demonstrate that you're independent enough to think "outside the box." Commuter traffic is even more aggressive than you had expected, but you stay on high alert for the dumb stunts of other motorists. You're conscientious about bike upkeep, and your headlights and taillights are working. You do your part to be more conspicuous by wearing your high-viz jacket and white helmet, not following behind trucks or busses, and always maintaining a minimum following distance of three seconds.

As you ride through an intersection, you notice a car ahead on your right, but you're far enough back that the guy driving can easily see you in his left mirror. Besides, you have the right-of-way, so you maintain position and traffic speed.

Three seconds later, you're startled when the driver suddenly brakes and swerves left into your lane. You barely manage to brake quickly enough to avoid getting sideswiped. You are angered by the sudden lane change without signaling, so you beep your horn. The guy looks in his rear view mirror but doesn't seem to comprehend why you're beeping at him.

If you had been more aware of the situation, you would have noticed the parked car ahead. There aren't three traffic lanes here, but two traffic lanes and a parking strip. The driver might have thought he was in a third traffic lane and panicked when he noticed a car ahead not moving. Rather than brake, he swerved left. It's very likely he never looked in his mirrors.

At any time in traffic, about half of the other drivers will not observe a motorcycle, no matter how conspicuous. To avoid collisions, you must constantly scan the situation ahead, spot potential problems in advance, and take the initiative to get out of the way. Having the right-of-way does not prevent another motorist from swerving into your path. And it's little consolation to be right when you're the one who gets trucked off to the ER.

In this situation, you should have predicted that the driver would suddenly panic and swerve into your lane. You could have avoided the conflict by simply opening up a space for the other driver. Don't expect thanks for your actions, but you can mentally pat yourself on the back for being in control of the situation.

Midtown Mayhem

Reading traffic in a big city is a fine art.

One of the problems with living in the big city is that you have to survive heavy traffic to get out of town and get on the back roads you prefer to ride. Today, you're about halfway across town, approaching a confusing series of intersections. There's a girl on a bicycle waiting to cross, and you know that sometimes bicyclists and pedestrians will dart across the street against the light. This bicyclist seems to be waiting for the light to change.

You know that about half of the other drivers on the road will not see a motorcycle, so you stay alert for what's happening and then position yourself to stay out of the way. An orange truck is almost hanging out in the lane, but you predict that the driver's more interested in making a turn and won't back up. You're more concerned about that black van ahead waiting to turn left across traffic. The driver may not see you and might attempt a quick turn as soon as the cars get by. You move over toward the right side of the lane to add a space cushion, shift down a gear, and ease on some front brake to prepare for a quick stop if needed. But the van driver waits for you to get through the intersection, and you ease off the brake and continue.

There's a commercial moving truck parked ahead, and you predict that it will stay put, but the car ahead on your right will ease over into the left lane to get around it. You suspect that the car driver doesn't see you. There's no problem. You just dab on a little front brake to open up some space and let the driver in.

You were smart to monitor that left-turning black van because that's the most likely accident scenario for a motorcyclist in city traffic. By being aware of the unfolding situation, you just make small adjustments to avoid having to attempt difficult emergency maneuvers. It's going to be a good day.

Motorcycle Sandwich

Don't let your guard down just because nothing scary has happened since breakfast.

You've finally found enough vacation time for a quick cross-country trip, and you're settling into the routine of riding all day on the freeway. Traffic is faster and more aggressive than in previous years, but you're starting to relax as you get into the mental groove of freeway riding. You're a respectable distance behind the truck ahead, so you glance down to check the GPS, odometer, and fuel gauge.

Suddenly, you notice a blur in your peripheral vision and look up to see a van squeezing into your lane and the driver braking. You quickly roll off the throttle and reach for the brakes, but you're closing fast on the van's bumper. Adding to your terror, you hear the screech of tires behind you. You manage to brake just in time, but suddenly there is a big jolt as the car behind you slams into your bike and knocks it forward. You're thrown off the bike; luckily, other drivers manage to avoid running over you. As everything stops spinning, you find yourself on the ground with faces peering down at you. You're instantly aware that your ride is over.

Things happen quickly on high-speed highways. At 70 mph, you're covering more than 100 feet per second. In this situation, you should have been more aware of the vehicles around you and taken action to increase your space cushion. There are several reasons to never follow immediately behind a view-blocking truck. And it was a bad time to divert your attention to secondary details. The van driver may have been surprised by a lane closure but hadn't allowed enough following distance for the situation. It's possible she didn't realize you were there. If you had been more attentive to the situation, you would very likely have seen the van moving over, and you could have swerved onto the left shoulder to escape.

Neighborhood Dogs

You need to be smarter than Fido.

It's a warm afternoon in the neighborhood, and you're cruising along minding your own business. A dog suddenly trots out into the street with his eyes on you. You know that some dogs like to chase motorcycles, but you're not sure about this dog. His ears are back and his tail is down, signs of aggression, but he isn't baring any teeth or snarling.

Just as you get close, he turns to chase the bike and is running alongside. He doesn't seem intent on biting you, just having some fun. Now he sprints up to snap at your front tire and gets too close. Your front wheel bounces over the dog, you lose balance, and the bike comes crashing down. The dog whimpers and runs off, leaving you to deal with the damaged bike and scuffed riding gear.

One successful dog-evasion tactic is to slow way down when you see a dog in the road or a dog sprinting toward you from a yard, to give the dog the idea that there is no need to hurry. Then, suddenly accelerate. Most motorcycles can accelerate faster than a canine. It's not smart to attempt to kick a dog because the dog very likely has quicker reflexes than you do. And an aggressive large dog has teeth that can penetrate armored riding gear.

Loose dogs are a big problem in some neighborhoods. Any size dog can topple over a bike by darting in front of it. If you encounter the same aggressive dog time after time, it will quickly learn your tricks. It is best to try talking as politely as possible to the dog's owner or, if necessary, making a complaint to the animal-control office. You would be doing other motorcyclists—and possibly the neighbors—a favor. If you don't have the time or interest to deal with the dog's owner, avoid this street.

Night Riding

It's hard to not stare at bright lights.

There's a club rally in the next state this weekend, but you don't have any vacation days left. You decide that you can still make the rally by Saturday noon if you leave after work on Friday and ride all night. You realize it's going to be colder at night, so you put on your electric jacket liner and winter gloves. And you snap on a clear face shield and coat it inside with an anti-fog chemical.

You haven't done much night riding, so there are some surprises. First, you didn't realize how the asphalt pavement outside of cities can be so dark. Your stock headlight doesn't illuminate enough to really light up the road, especially those areas where new asphalt has been applied. You're glad the painted lines are still visible, giving you better clues about your position in the lane.

Your biggest problem is when an oncoming car comes along. The headlights are a shock as they suddenly loom out of the dark; then, when the car passes, you're blind for several seconds. That really scares you because you know there are often surface hazards on highways, including jagged pieces of truck tire tread, vehicle parts, and even roadkill.

Night riding requires some different tactics, as well as different accessories. If you decide to ride at night, consider installing more powerful lights. But be sure to check the laws to stay legal. Don't forget about lights and reflectors on the back of your machine to help other motorists see you.

One helpful tactic for oncoming cars is to make a point of not focusing on approaching headlights. Instead, focus on the fog line, the painted line at the right edge of your lane. That allows your central vision to stay in "night" mode, while your less sensitive peripheral vision soaks up the bright light. After the oncoming vehicle has passed, you can refocus your central vision on the road ahead.

FOCUS ON
FOG LINE

No Zone Neglect

It's never smart to park in a trucker's blind spots.

In light traffic on an urban arterial, you notice a large truck gaining on you in the center lane. You're not concerned about riding alongside a big truck because you know the driver saw you as he pulled alongside. You ease on some throttle to maintain the speed of traffic.

Suddenly, without warning the truck starts to pull over into your lane. At first, you thought it was just the driver not paying attention, but the truck keeps coming, and you are forced over onto the shoulder to avoid being hit. You're furious, and you accelerate up alongside the cab honking your horn and shouting. The driver seems confused at your actions, but of course there's nothing he can do. The big mistake here was assuming the truck driver knew where you were. At first, he was gaining on you, so he might have predicted that he had passed you.

But staying abreast of the truck put you in his blind spot. A driver's views in the mirrors are very limited, and it's easy to lose track of a motorcycle. Even if the driver signals, you aren't in a good position to see the lights blinking. That's why the areas alongside trucks are called the "No Zone."

To prevent collisions, be aware of the developing situation and take evasive action early. It's never smart to pace a large vehicle. You can predict that a trucker on an urban arterial might be looking for a delivery address or cross street and get out of his way early. For example, you could have accelerated and moved into the center lane to position yourself in front of the truck where the driver could see you better. Or, you could have dropped back to a position where a lane change by the trucker wouldn't endanger you.

Oily Corners

Commercial trucks are notorious for leaking fluids.

On a trip to the Northwest, you are really enjoying exploring the secondary highways with lots of curves and not as much traffic. You see a logging truck coming up fast from behind, and when it appears that the truck driver really has the hammer down, you move over and let him on by. You're insulted by the aggressive driving and close pass, but you realize that log truck drivers are focused on moving logs, not on avoiding dawdling motorcyclists.

A couple of turns later, your tires suddenly step sideways and your heart leaps into your throat. Fortunately, your muscle memory is sufficient to maintain a steady throttle and not snap it closed. The bike slips sideways for a few feet, the tires hook up again, and you manage to keep the bike upright. But now your heart is racing, your adrenaline is surging, and you're curious about what just happened.

As you observe the surface more carefully, you realize that the outbound trucks must be spilling diesel fuel from their overfilled saddle tanks as the drivers rush back to the logging roads. You ran over such a diesel spill while leaned over in the corner. Some trucks (and more than a few busses) also dribble continuous streams of lubricating oil on the pavement.

Of course, it's unconscionable that trucking firms would allow their vehicles to spill fuel, engine oil, and hydraulic fluid on the pavement, but it's a fact of life out in the country away from the big cities. A well-worn leaker is not going to attract much attention. It's up to you to be aware of what's happening and avoid the slick stuff.

You may be able to spot the dark color or multicolored sheen of oil on the surface, but your best tactic is to avoid those areas where such contaminants tend to collect. Fuel tends to spill out the filler caps, so any escaped fuel will tend to spread close to the wheel tracks toward the outside of a curve. Lubricating oils tend to drip in the center of the lane. A cornering line outside of the wheel tracks is less likely to be lubricated. You can also observe where a constant stream of trucks is turning off. There will be fewer diesel spills on the return trip, since the tanks will then be less full.

You must constantly be alert to larger vehicles, even on roads that are otherwise quiet. You were wise to pull over and let the truck go by, to avoid being pushed faster than you feel comfortable. But you must also maintain your awareness of surface hazards.

One-way Weasels

Watch out for sleepy drivers on one-way streets.

You've been planning a trip for weeks, and today's the day. Last night, you checked the bike over and loaded it up. This morning, you're working your way out of town through commuter traffic as you mentally review your trip plan. You move to the left lane of a one-way street to get around a driver who's creeping along in the right lane. You'll be passing her in the intersection.

But before you can get around, the driver suddenly swerves left across your path, headed for a side street. You immediately roll off the gas, squeeze the clutch, and apply both brakes just short of a skid. You manage to slow enough to just miss the car's rear bumper. The driver continues her left turn and motors off, oblivious to the crash she almost caused.

You're fuming under your helmet at the carelessness of a driver making a left turn from the right lane, until you theorize that the sleepy driver might have thought she was on a two-way street with no oncoming traffic. If that's the case, she certainly wouldn't have expected someone to pass her in the intersection. You also replay the near-collision in your head and realize that you were riding in her blind spot entering the intersection. You're a little embarrassed to admit that you were partially to blame. You need to focus on the situation and not be daydreaming about the roads ahead of you.

Being skillful at hard braking really paid off in this situation. You were able to avoid a nasty collision. But you might have predicted the driver would turn left at the intersection and stayed farther behind. Accelerating into an intersection is almost never a good tactic because increasing speed boosts forward energy and lengthens stopping distance.

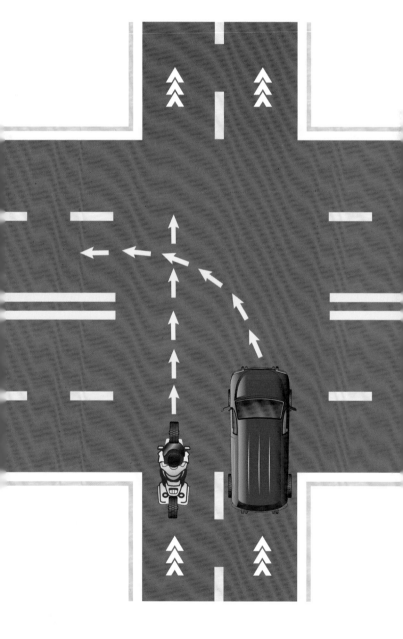

Over Your Head

It's important to ride your own ride, especially when you're in fast company.

You've been invited to go for a ride with some motorcyclists you met at the dealership. You don't know these riders, but they all ride bikes similar to yours, are in your same age bracket, and wear quality riding gear. Showing up for the ride today, you're looking forward to socializing with them. You're a bit surprised when one of the leaders suddenly announces "Let's go" and starts his engine, without any explanation of where the ride is going or any road rules. You quickly get your helmet and gloves on, but find yourself at the back of the pack as the leaders accelerate down the street and turn off onto a narrow road into the hills.

The group turns out to be a lot more aggressive than you had expected, riding at elevated speeds through residential areas and carving around corners as if in a race. You try to keep up because you don't want them to think of you as less skilled. You just tuck in behind the rider ahead and try to stay with him.

Suddenly, as you lean over hard into a tight corner, your rear tire drops off the edge of the pavement. Instantly, the bike is down and sliding. Luckily, the bike slides into the grass without too much damage.

Thanks to your gear you aren't seriously injured, but you're extremely embarrassed.

Although it can be fun to ride with a group, you should understand that some groups can be very competitive, and their rides can be more like races than social events. Be aware that riders at the tail end of any group must ride faster than those in the front to catch up. It's never smart to try hanging with a group just by following the bike ahead. You need to ride your own ride, especially when you're in the company of riders who may have a much higher skill level than you or who are willing to take greater risks. It's better to fall back and manage your own ride at a pace you find comfortable than to ride over your head and risk a crash.

Parking-lot Darters

You can expect other drivers to ignore the traffic rules in parking lots.

You need to stop off at the grocery store on your way home to pick up some milk. Big parking lots always make you nervous because drivers seem to pull so many dumb and dangerous maneuvers. You're watching carefully for pedestrians walking in the lane and for drivers who cut across the lanes. You scrutinize the parked cars to spot any signs that someone is about to pull out, including backup lights flashing or a wheel starting to rotate.

You notice a white car starting to pull out, and you're shocked that the driver of the car ahead of you doesn't brake. The driver barely manages to squeak by the white car without scraping. You ease on the front brake to be prepared for anything. Sure enough, as the car ahead clears the bumper of the white car, the driver gasses it and darts out into your path. You ease on a bit more front brake to slow and stay out of the way.

Although you might think that drivers in parking lots would follow the same rules as on the street, there really aren't any traffic rules on private property, and there is seldom any enforcement. You just have to stay on high alert and be prepared to get out of the way of whatever happens. You should scan adjacent lanes as well as the one you're in, to spot drivers about to dart across the lanes between parked cars.

You should be especially aware of any vehicle that must be backed out of a parking spot. The driver is unlikely to have a clear view of the lane. Watch for people just getting into vehicles or the backup lights momentarily flickering as the driver shifts into reverse. Your best technique for avoiding a collision is to be aware of what's happening and move out of the way.

Passing Panic

It's seldom wise to pass over a double yellow.

It's starting to look like an outstanding day for a Saturday ride. The weather is cloudy-bright and warm, and you've ridden far enough out of town that traffic is sparse. You're not in a hurry, but it feels good to ride at a brisk pace. The ride was going fine until you came up behind a slow-moving truck towing a boat. The driver speeds up in the straights and then brakes for the curves. You'd like to pass, but the double yellow lines seem to go on for miles.

Finally, you've had enough. You monitor the road behind to make sure no one is about to pass you and look ahead to spot any oncoming vehicles or lurking patrol cars. You pull out far enough to see that there's no oncoming traffic and then crank up the throttle. You're still accelerating when suddenly the truck and trailer swerve left followed by the left-turn signal. You're shocked to realize the driver is making a left turn onto a side road you hadn't noticed.

With your path quickly being blocked off, your options are limited. There's just no room to brake. Rather than hit the trailer, you swerve left toward the greenery. The front wheel slams into the ditch and the bike cartwheels into the underbrush. You'll find out later—when you are released from the hospital—that your bike is a total loss. It's a painful and expensive lesson about not passing over the double yellow.

The crash is all the more painful because you did it to yourself while attempting an illegal pass. The truck driver isn't at fault, because you know it's legal in your state to turn left across the double yellow onto an existing road. What's more, the truck driver had good reason to assume that no one would be passing him in a no-passing zone.

In this situation, the truck driver turning off the road would have opened up the lane for you, making a pass unnecessary. Of course, you couldn't have known that. If the driver had not turned off, there very likely would have been a legal passing opportunity within the next few miles.

One tactic for dealing with the frustration of slow-moving drivers is to pull over and take a short break, then get back on the road and ride at your preferred pace to catch up.

Pendulous Passes

If you're going to pass, get prepared.

Your Sunday ride has been fun. The weather is warm and dry, and you're enjoying this secondary highway that snakes around cliffs and through the forest. You've ridden this road many times, so you have a pretty good idea of where it goes, where sight distance is limited, and where it's legal to pass.

At the moment, you're being held up by a slow-moving dump truck. Actually, the driver is doing almost the speed limit, but you'd like to get around before you reach a hilly section. You know there's a straight ahead where it's appropriate to pass if there's no oncoming traffic. So, as the road straightens out, you signal, take a quick glance in your mirrors, and roll on. You instantly realize you had neglected to shift down, so the bike accelerates sluggishly. You simply hold the throttle open and wait as the engine comes up in the power band.

Now, as you pull abreast of the truck, you realize there's an oncoming car, and it's approaching faster than you would have predicted. You quickly drop down a gear, accelerate, and manage to squeeze back in front of the truck. It's too close for comfort, and you're annoyed at the speeding oncoming driver.

Rather than being annoyed at the other driver, you should be annoyed at yourself for the sloppy pass. When you're ready to pass, drop down into an appropriate gear, then signal, glance behind, scrutinize the situation ahead, and make a decision. If it's appropriate to pass, accelerate quickly to limit the time you're hanging out in the opposing lane. And when pulling back into your lane, leave some space ahead of the vehicle being passed to avoid a conflict.

If the road ahead is not clear, or if you only realize there's opposing traffic after you've pulled out, abort the pass. Brake, signal, drop back, and pull back in line. Remember, two opposing vehicles moving at speeds of 60 mph are hurtling toward each other at a closing speed of 120 mph.

You should also be suspicious of vehicles that are out of place, such as a dump truck in a residential area or an eighteen-wheeler on a twisty back road. The driver may be looking for an address to make a delivery or just looking for a place to make a U-turn. It shouldn't be a surprise if the driver suddenly turns off into a driveway or onto a side road.

Poor Predicting

A bad guess can morph a near-miss into a collision.

You're on the way home from work. With the nicer weather, you've been riding the bike more and more. It's fast, fun, and maneuverable. You've installed a freeway blaster horn, not so obnoxious to wake up errant drivers, but to give them a "raspberry" after they do something stupid. And after a few months of commuting, you're getting pretty good at predicting what other drivers are going to do.

You're approaching an intersection where drivers often turn left to get to a big grocery store. When you see a truck pulling a huge trailer in the left-turn lane, you predict that the out-of-town driver will make a slow turn across your path and be late clearing the intersection.

Sure enough, the truck is slow to accelerate and is still turning as the signal light changes. You plan to swerve around just inches behind the trailer and blast your horn at the driver to hurry him along. You blip the throttle to announce your presence and accelerate as soon as the light turns green. Unfortunately for you, the truck driver panics when he sees you and jams on the brakes, bringing the truck and trailer to a complete stop blocking all three lanes. You try to swerve around the trailer, but there just isn't room. The bike bounces off the back corner of the trailer before you get the opportunity to blast your horn.

Attempts to outwit or embarrass other drivers can quickly backfire. And even if the other driver is at fault, a motorcyclist wins the ride in the ambulance more often than not. A visiting driver may not appreciate a quick signal light or an intersection requiring a tight turn. And although you correctly predicted the course of the truck, you may have failed to predict how much time and road space it takes to get a big trailer moving.

You can indignantly claim that it was the other driver's fault for failing to obey the traffic signal, but we know who made it happen, don't we? Rather than trying to pull stunts on other drivers, why not just cut them some slack? What's more, it's always a good idea to leave room for things to go wrong.

Problem Drivers

Some drivers are mentally unstable; others just hate motorcyclists.

Riding a secondary highway, you come up behind an erratic driver in a pickup truck. He speeds up to tailgate the car ahead, then slows for no apparent reason and drops back. He wanders around in the lane, sometimes driving halfway onto the shoulder or across the centerline. You suspect he is either intoxicated or having a medical problem. What's more, the mattresses in the back of the pickup don't appear to be secured very well. Other vehicles are collecting behind you, and you want to get around this guy before he causes a crash.

There's a short straight ahead, and although it's not a legal passing zone, you roll on the throttle and get around, pulling back into the right lane well ahead of the truck to avoid appearing to be overly aggressive. Suddenly, you hear a horn beeping behind you and check your mirrors. You're startled to see that the pickup driver has accelerated right up behind you, beeping his horn and waving a fist. To avoid getting rear-ended, you quickly pass the three cars ahead of you and keep on accelerating to get farther away from the craziness.

There's no lack of bad driving out there, and remember that about ten percent of the population has some sort of serious mental issue. Some people don't believe you have any right to use public roads, others choose to view passing as a put-down, and still others simply hate motorcyclists. A person's erratic driving behavior and the condition of the vehicle or load are clues about the driver's mental state.

When you realized you were too close to a problem driver, your tactic to separate yourself was good. However, making an illegal pass did not defuse the situation effectively. It might have been better to pull over and take a short break, allowing other drivers to deal with the problem guy.

Pushy Passengers

When carrying a passenger, you need to adjust your riding techniques.

Most of the time, you ride by yourself, but once in a while your significant other expresses a willingness to join you for a ride. The weather this weekend is turning out sunny, and the time has come to carry a passenger for a day.

You understand the importance of protective gear, so you dig out a spare helmet that fits, gloves, and a fabric riding jacket. Since your passenger is not very familiar with motorcycling, you explain what's going to happen, how to climb on and off the bike, and the hand signals to use when there is a need for a break. You take it easy for the first hour while your passenger gets acquainted with the feel of the bike. Then, after a rest break, you gradually work up to your usual speeds and lean angles.

While riding a quiet section of country road, you notice a deer grazing ahead and ease off the throttle. But suddenly, as you get close, the deer snaps into action, leaping out of the ditch onto the road. You immediately reach for the brake and squeeze progressively harder, but you're not prepared for your passenger to slam into your back and push you forward. You have to limit your braking to prevent being pushed forward onto the tank. Luckily, the deer makes a last-second leap out of your path, but it could just as easily have been a collision and a tumble down the pavement.

You were correct in providing protective gear and explaining what to expect during the ride. And it was a good tactic to start out at a modest pace to allow your passenger time to adapt. But when carrying a passenger, you must adjust your riding techniques to allow for the extra weight. Expect longer stopping distances and more rear brake performance because of the increased weight on the rear wheel. Rather than working up to your usual solo speed, you're better off keeping your speed more conservative for the entire ride.

When you do spot a hazard, such as deer alongside the road, consider braking immediately to reduce speed rather than just rolling off the throttle and covering the brake lever. That allows you to decelerate over a longer distance, dissipating the forward energy more gradually and predictably. If you regularly carry the same passenger, it's not a bad idea to practice aggressive stops with the passenger on board.

Racer Road Respect

Just because it's a nice curvy road doesn't mean it's your personal racetrack.

Like many other riders, you probably have some favorite public roads you like to enjoy at an aggressive pace. It's especially fun when the weather is pleasant, the pavement is clean and dry, and there isn't any traffic. You can concentrate on controlling the bike, smoothly leaning into corners, adjusting lean angle with the throttle, and practicing delayed apex cornering lines. It's like having your own personal racetrack without having to pay for a closed track. Since you know you're going to push a bit, you wear your best protective gear.

You're enjoying one of your favorite "racer roads" at warp speed, when you round a blind turn to find a tourist making a U-turn in the road. You attempt to get the bike upright and transition from throttle to brakes, but there just isn't time or space to get your speed down. You brake hard, then veer off onto the gravel shoulder, where the bike goes down. You avoid a collision, but your bike is damaged, and you're in pain and suspect that you have some broken ribs.

It's a dangerous trap to think of any road as your personal racetrack. Public roads may sometimes appear to be reasonably free of traffic, surface hazards, and other obstructions, but you can't depend on any public road to be completely safe. Expect the pavement to be less than perfect and other road users—including tourists and wild animals—to get in your way. If you really want to ride fast, the safest venue is a closed track where there are few hazards, and everyone is going in the same direction.

You may think the speed limits posted on public roads are "ridiculously slow," but if you ride at the posted speeds you are much less likely to have any crashes. If you choose to ride faster than the posted limits—and to break the law, which I am not advising—you need to be *very* good at predicting and avoiding hazards (and tickets!).

Railroad Traps

Those shiny rails and slippery planks can be dangerous, especially if the road curves across.

You've decided to take the day off and go for a ride. The weather hasn't turned out to be sunny and warm, but at least it's not raining. You've been meaning to ride this secondary highway for several years, and today's the day. It's not a bad road, but there are lots of surface problems that are spoiling the ride.

When you come upon two railroad tracks in a curve, you're momentarily stumped. You've read somewhere that you don't have to do anything special when crossing railroad tracks, but those wooden aprons look awfully rough and the steel rails are smooth and slippery. You're wondering if you should swerve over to the left and cross the rails in more of a straight line. But before you can decide, you're there. The bike bounces up onto a fresh asphalt area and clatters across the rails. You feel both tires slip sideways a bit on the steel, and that makes you nervous.

If the bike is leaning at all, it's more likely the tires will slip sideways on the rails or on the wooden aprons. It's best to cross any shiny rails at the maximum angle, 90 degrees if that's possible, to reduce the side forces. A wide angle also helps prevent a tire from hooking on a groove or hole. So, yes, in a situation like this, you should move over toward the centerline to allow crossing the tracks at a wider angle and in a straighter line.

Wood planks next to the rails can be uneven, loose, cracked, or rotted, so your concern was not misplaced. Wood aprons can be very slippery when wet, so it helps to keep the bike vertical when crossing them if it's been raining.

Take extra caution if the road rises up to cross tracks that are on an elevated roadbed because traction will temporarily decrease as the bike lifts up on the suspension. But don't squander so much of your attention on the surface hazards that you ignore an approaching train!

Rainy-day Slipups

Riding on rain-slick surfaces takes special skill.

When gas prices soared to an all-time high, you decided to use your motorcycle for commuting to work whenever the weather allowed. The weather has been sunny and bright for the past two weeks, but the clouds rolled in this afternoon and now it's starting to rain. There doesn't seem to be any choice but to suit up and point the bike toward home. You have the right gear to stay warm and dry, but you're nervous about riding in traffic on the slick surface.

You're a bit surprised at the aggressiveness of other drivers. You leave plenty of space ahead of you to avoid having to do any sudden braking. You know from experience that there is always a rash of collisions when it starts to rain.

When you roll on a bit more throttle on an upgrade, you feel the rear tire slip. You panic and roll off, which seems to make it worse. Suddenly, the rear wheel is fishtailing from side to side, threatening to throw you off. You manage to calm down and ease back on the throttle, and the rear tire regains traction. But now you're really spooked by the sudden loss of traction, and you can't avoid thoughts of what it would be like to go down on a busy freeway.

It is true that there is typically a rash of crashes when it first starts to rain. A dry road surface gets coated with oil droppings, dirt, and other debris, which mix with newly fallen rainwater to form a slippery goo. It takes about a half hour of steady rain to wash the debris away.

It's always wise to check the weather forecast to determine whether or not riding the bike to work is advisable. In this situation, you could have delayed your homeward commute for a half hour to allow more time for the fresh rain to wash away the goo. When you are riding in the rain, it's best to stay in the wheel tracks of other vehicles and avoid the center of the lane where oil collects.

Rash Righties

If you can't see the other driver, he or she probably can't see you.

You're on your way home from work, riding in the right lane of a four-lane arterial. You're aware of the hazard of getting rear-ended by tired commuters, so you maintain lots of following distance behind the car ahead. You're gradually slowing here because the signal light at the next intersection is red.

Then, suddenly and unexpectedly, a car accelerates out of the alley into your path, turning right. Before you can reach for the brake lever, the bike's front tire taps a dent into the left rear door of the car. The driver stops, clearly surprised at the collision, and repeats the well-worn phrase, "Are you all right? I didn't see you." You and the driver exchange information and continue on your separate ways without involving a formal investigation.

Actually, the driver in this situation very likely could not see you because there was a power pole blocking the view. If you can't see the other driver, she probably can't see you. She may have assumed that the lane was available because you were so far behind the vehicle ahead, and you were riding so slowly. You were unexpected. You can flip a coin here as to who's at fault, but it would probably be wiser to fill out an accident report.

You should have been more aware of the situation and realized the driver was waiting to pull out. You could have slowed enough to allow the other driver to turn. And, you could have moved to the left side of the lane—or even moved to the left lane—to improve your chance of being seen.

Whenever the situation is unclear, you should be covering the front brake lever to allow for a quick slowdown or stop. When watching to see whether a car is starting to move, the earliest clue is the top of the front wheel, which moves twice as fast as the bumper.

Revolting Rails

It doesn't take much shiny steel to cause a slide out.

You're exploring the city today, wandering down side streets with a variety of odd businesses. There's not much traffic here because most drivers know exactly where they are going. You're gawking, not hurrying, but there are some areas where the pavement is so uneven you stand on the pegs to absorb the bumps.

As you are rounding a sweeping right-hand curve, you notice some old railroad rails buried in the surface, but you figure the rails are just one more surface problem to negotiate. You maintain speed and lean angle.

It's a shock when your front tire slides out on a pair of rails that are close together. The bike does a slow-motion fall and slides off on a tangent to the left. You tumble off unhurt, but you've lost a mirror and scratched up the front fender. You're more surprised than angry. You realize the rails were left over from some old industrial sidings and were just left exposed. Passing car tires have kept them polished smooth and shiny, and the pair of rails close together encouraged your tire to slide sideways.

Single-vehicle crashes are becoming more common than two-vehicle collisions these days, and lots of slide-outs are caused by surface hazards such as rails and pavement edges. Some rails are especially tricky because they have deep slots that can catch your tire and redirect it, making it very difficult to maintain balance.

Treat all rail crossings with respect, especially those in curves. In this situation, you could have kept more to the right and crossed the multiple rails with the bike vertical rather than leaned over.

Right-turn Reprobates

Just because other drivers get in your way doesn't mean you are blameless.

You've been exploring a favorite country highway that's fun except for the occasional small towns. Other drivers seem to dawdle unnecessarily, and you're anxious to get through traffic and get back up to speed.

Just as you are accelerating through an intersection, a driver on your right pulls out, making a right turn. You quickly gas it and manage to squeeze through the narrow gap, but that apparently startles the driver, who jams on the brakes and beeps his horn.

You're angered that the other driver would make a turn so close in front of you. And you're sure he must have seen your headlight and bright-colored gear. In this situation, even though you had the legal right-of-way, you should have predicted that the driver would make a turn and adjusted your speed accordingly to avoid a conflict. Furthermore, passing the other car after it had turned is very likely illegal.

A big part of surviving traffic is being constantly aware of the situation so that you can take evasive action early to avoid collisions. You should be aware that even if you have taken steps to be more conspicuous, a driver who is not expecting to see a motorcycle may not comprehend that you are there. It's more than a matter of not seeing you: the driver has to pass along the image to the conscious parts of his or her brain.

Let's also note the difficulty of a driver correctly judging your approaching distance and speed. A narrow motorcycle will seem farther away and slower than a larger vehicle. And if you are riding faster than surrounding traffic, a driver can easily misjudge your speed.

It's seldom wise to accelerate through an intersection. In this situation, you managed to squeeze through the gap and avoid a collision, but that was more luck than skill. The better tactic is to ease on some front brake when approaching an intersection or a questionable situation, which will help to reduce speed and give you a better chance of a successful evasive maneuver.

Road Debris

Never be so focused on making time that you aren't watching for surface hazards.

You're out for a leisurely weekend ride in the country. You've ridden this same road many times, so you know its twists and turns, and the likely places to pass slower traffic. You've been following a slow-moving dump truck for several miles, and you're anxious to get around it. You know there is a straight ahead, although there are a couple of narrow bridges. You move up close behind the truck and shift down a gear so that, if there's no oncoming traffic, you can swing over for a quick pass between the two bridges.

Just as you're about to roll on, you hear a loud thump and see a large rock tumbling out from under the truck right into your path. Before you can take any evasive action, your front wheel hits the rock, the front end is almost jerked out of your grasp, and you hear a loud pop as the tire instantly deflates. You gradually ease off the throttle but avoid braking as the bike wobbles and swerves. You're barely able to get it over to the side of the road without dropping it or hitting the sides of the bridge, and you're shaking like a leaf. On inspection, you find your front rim split apart from impacting the rock. It will be hours before you can arrange for a buddy to transport the bike home in his pickup truck.

What set you up for the blowout were following too closely behind the truck and focusing on passing rather than maintaining your awareness of other hazards, including debris kicked aside by the truck's tires. Following so closely means you don't have any reaction time, even if you see a problem. Although you intended to get around the truck, you didn't have to pass right then and there. It might be a good idea to stay far enough behind the vehicle ahead to allow you to see and avoid the hazards, including vehicles pulling out of side roads, wild animals, potholes, and yes, big rocks in the road.

Road Gorp

A little rainfall can turn the surface into a slippery mess.

It's Saturday morning, the sun is shining, and you eagerly check your oil and tire pressures in preparation for a great ride. The weather for the past couple of weeks hasn't been wet, just gray and gloomy, so you're ready for a good ride on a dry road under a blue sky. The weather prediction is for a storm to blow in tomorrow. You zip into your fabric riding gear with its impact pads and breathable waterproof fabric.

By noon, you're miles from home, having ridden a series of your favorite curving roads that were as traffic-free as you had hoped. You plan on a lunch stop at your favorite roadside café halfway up the mountain. It's a bit of a surprise when you arrive at the café to feel raindrops starting to patter down and realize that the storm is arriving earlier than predicted. It's not raining hard, but you know it will be, so you reluctantly cut the ride short, skip lunch, and hurry toward home.

Your more direct route takes you back into city traffic on a major arterial. The surface is surprisingly slick. Crossing a steel construction plate, your rear tire spins up momentarily. And when you brake for a red light, both tires start to slide. You manage to keep the bike upright, but only by allowing the tires to roll halfway into the crosswalk. You can feel your boot soles slipping around as you gingerly hold the bike upright. By the time you return to your garage, you're really paranoid about the slick streets.

During periods when there is no rain, various contaminants such as grease, oil, and pulverized debris collect on the pavement surface. When it first starts to rain, the contaminants mix with water to form a very slippery goo or "road gorp." It takes a half hour or more of steady rain to wash the "gorp" off the pavement and allow reasonable traction.

Rather than hurry home, you should have ridden more conservatively on the slick surfaces. Better yet, you could have enjoyed a very leisurely lunch to allow time for the new rain to wash away the accumulated contaminants. By the time you got back into city traffic, the surface would have been much less slippery.

Road Sharks

Don't let aggressive drivers take a bite out of your ride.

You're cruising home from the Saturday breakfast meeting. The weather isn't very cooperative—it's starting to rain. You're in no hurry, but your habit is to ride a little faster than the average speed of traffic. You know that crashes can occur quickly on the superslab, so you scan the situation far ahead and watch for any signs of a problem. You're not turning off, so you stay out of the right lane. You are next to a loaded logging truck that is flinging dirty water and mud, so you decide to change one lane to the right to get farther away.

You glance over your shoulder to ensure there's no one in your blind spot, then signal and start to move over. But suddenly the driver of a large SUV swerves into the same lane— right on top of you. The situation suddenly gets worse when a car ahead of you slows down and the SUV driver brakes hard to avoid a rear-ender. You transition from throttle to brakes as smoothly and quickly as possible and barely manage to avoid ramming the SUV by lane splitting over the white dots.

You're angered that the SUV driver didn't look or signal before changing lanes. His move was so sudden and so aggressive that you have to believe that he was simply bulling his way over without regard for your safety.

It's always smart to look far ahead in traffic to spot problems early. If you had been aware of the situation all around you, you might have predicted that the SUV driver would change lanes and then delayed your lane change.

Signaling your intentions may not encourage aggressive drivers to avoid moving into your path, but it's the law, and it might help in some situations. If you think back to your lane-change technique, you may note that you didn't signal until you actually started to move over. You should always signal at least 3 seconds prior to any move. So, if you're planning a lane change, signal first, then look, then move if the situation is amenable.

Rolling Stops

It's always a good idea to make a complete stop for red lights or Stop signs.

You're on a two-week trip, and today's ride has been exhausting. You pull off the freeway to find lodging for the night. You find yourself on a one-way street that T's into a cross street, with traffic controlled by a signal light.

The right lane is for right turns only. You notice the right-turn arrow is red, but you recall that right turns against a red light are permitted in this state. You're tired enough that you'd prefer to roll around the corner without having to come to a complete stop. So, you slow down, look for cross traffic, and turn right without stopping. But, just as you are making your turn, an oncoming car turns left in front of you. You grab for the brakes to avoid a collision, but braking with the bike leaned over upsets balance and it crashes onto its side.

As you struggle to get the bike righted, you realize that there is oncoming traffic from the off-ramp, and apparently those vehicles had a green light. You're embarrassed to realize you almost caused a collision. You should have come to a complete stop and waited for a green light.

If you were thinking more clearly and scrutinizing the situation, you might have spotted the sign prohibiting turns on a red light. Even if there wasn't a sign, it's never a good idea to roll through a stop, whether controlled by a Stop sign or a traffic light. As you discovered, if traffic unexpectedly gets in your way, it's hard to keep the bike balanced. In states where turns from a stop are allowed, the caveat is that you must come to a complete stop before proceeding and ensure there is a break in traffic to allow you to merge.

It's especially important to make complete stops when riding in a group. Lazier or less skilled riders may prefer to turn without stopping, and that encourages following riders to do the same. One rider back in the pack deciding to make a legal stop can cause confusion. To avoid potential rear-enders, everyone must plan on making a complete foot-down stop. The only exception is when the group is being escorted by an on-duty police officer and he blocks traffic.

Rubber Alligators

Slabs of truck tire tread can snap at you if you're not prepared.

You're on the way home from a great weekend at the races, and you're hyped. But, for this secondary highway on a Sunday afternoon, you're amazed at the truck traffic. You know that truckers have a very limited view in their mirrors, so you stay out of their blind spots and maintain a speed that doesn't encourage any truckers to pass you.

You move to the left lane to get around a gaggle of trucks. But just as you are about to pass them, the last truck in line suddenly swerves over in front of you. You're not sure whether the driver saw you but didn't care or really didn't see you at all. You're a little miffed at the sudden lane change, so you flip on your high beam. Suddenly, you notice an acrid smell and hear a thumping sound—you realize that one of the tires on the truck's trailer is about to disintegrate.

You roll off, but before you can open up much separation, there is a loud hollow *whump* and a long section of tire tread is flung back toward you. It's huge and flailing around, and it suddenly slams into the front of your bike, shattering your front fender, raking the right leg of your riding pants, and knocking off the right saddlebag. You ease the bike toward the shoulder to inspect the damage. Your front fender is in tatters, one leg of your pants is seriously abraded, and the right saddlebag is gone. Looking back, you see the remnants of your saddlebag and gear being pulverized by a passing truck.

Truck tires do disintegrate, and some of the massive treads are reinforced with steel wires. Not only are these "rubber alligators" big and heavy, the jagged edges of the wires can easily slice through plastic or leather. Your best protection against being knocked down or chewed up is to avoid riding close alongside or behind a truck, especially if you detect any abnormal thumping or the odor of burning rubber.

Rude Runners

Expect impatient drivers to bull their way through intersections.

You're returning home from the hardware store with some fasteners for that loose porch railing. Traffic is busy on the street, so you watch for other vehicles that might get in your way. You're especially concerned about the oncoming cars in the left turn lane.

It's a surprise when a pickup truck comes zooming into the intersection from your left and then stops. You manage to ease on the brakes to prevent a rear-ender, but the aggressive move by the other driver is rude. What's more, if you had rear-ended the truck, you could have been held responsible for the crash.

You were wise to watch for other vehicles on a collision path. And left-turning vehicles are a significant hazard for motorcyclists. But don't forget that a left-turner might appear from your left, not just from the opposing left-turn lane.

Some drivers see you but are so rude and impatient they will just bull you out of the way. Some drivers see you but don't believe that a motorcycle has the same legal rights as a car or truck. And some drivers will fail to notice a motorcycle in traffic because they are not thinking about motorcycles. Even eye contact with another driver does not ensure that he or she will not get in your way.

In the event of a collision between a bike and a larger vehicle, the impact forces work against the bike. And since a motorcyclist doesn't have injury-prevention features such as crumple zones, air bags, and safety belts, a bike rider is much more likely to be injured in a collision than a car or truck driver. So, even when you have the legal right-of-way, it's essential to figure out what's happening and get out of the way.

Sandy Springs

Watch for leftover sand on your first springtime ride.

It's been a long, cold winter, and with the temperatures finally starting to warm up, you're itching for a ride. You've checked your tires, changed the oil, and disconnected the automatic battery charger for a day to make sure the battery is still healthy. The day isn't exactly warm, but the sun is shining and you're ready to go.

After several months of not riding, it feels a bit strange to be suited up in your gear, but your control skills quickly come back. You have to think harder to recall motorcycle-specific hazards, such as the grease strip in the center of the lane, slippery steel construction plates, and left-turning drivers who might fail to notice you. It's great to enjoy the performance of a motorcycle, and you head off onto some country roads you know will provide an entertaining ride.

Approaching a downhill right-hander, you suddenly panic when you see loose gravel on the pavement. You roll off the throttle and dab on the rear brake. But as you lean the bike over, the rear tire suddenly loses traction and jerks to the left. In your panic, you squeeze the clutch and ease on some front brake. But the bike slides out, falls on its right side, and slides off toward the opposing ditch. Thanks to your riding gear, you aren't seriously hurt, but your bike is a mess.

In climates or altitudes where icy roads are sanded in the wintertime, it's important for a motorcyclist to be aware of the leftover sand in the springtime. Although some maintenance crews sweep up the sand and fine gravel, others simply allow traffic to eventually push most of it off the pavement. Of course, on less popular roads, the loose sand will take much longer to dissipate.

Sand or gravel will appear as a rougher texture or possibly a darker color. You'll typically find it on slopes and at the sides of the connecting lanes at intersections. When you see loose sand in a corner, it's essential to slow down early to get the bike more vertical and to choose a line that puts your tire on the most tractable areas. If you feel your tires start to slide on loose sand, it's best to hold a steady throttle and avoid the brakes.

Side-street Scrapes

Side streets can lull you into a false sense of security.

You're returning home from your first Sunday ride of the season. The spring weather was pleasantly balmy, and traffic thinned out once you turned off the superslab. Now that you're away from the business of traffic, you can relax and savor the last few minutes of the ride. The bike performed well, and maybe you can squeeze in a quick wash before putting it away.

Then you see a curious glint of sunlight reflecting off one of the parked cars, and you realize one of the cars is starting to move. The driver is pulling away from the curb without looking. You transition to the brakes to avoid a collision, and the driver continues down the street, unaware that you took the initiative to get out of the way even though you had the right-of-way.

Side streets can lull you into a false sense of security because nothing seems to be happening. When someone pulls out of a parking space, backs out of a driveway, or makes a quick U-turn, it can be a surprise.

You were wise to keep your attention on the situation and catch the insignificant clue that something was about to happen. It's best to keep your speed down on those "quiet" side streets so that you can more easily brake to avoid a child running into the street or swerve to avert a collision with a driver veering away from an inattentive bicyclist.

Side-street Sideswipe

Just because you don't see anyone coming doesn't mean they aren't about to hit you.

You're approaching a cross-town arterial from a side street, following a pickup truck. The arterial is one lane in each direction, with a center divider, so there's no risk of a car crossing directly at you or of a

left-turning car swerving across your path. You're wary of people suddenly opening car doors into traffic, so you leave lots of room on both sides. To get up to traffic speed, you'll need to accelerate as you make your turn. But, just as you're braking to a stop, a car darts off the arterial from your left, its tires squealing. The car sideswipes the bike before you can do anything, and the driver roars off without stopping. You can't even get a license plate number. Luckily, the car only scrapes the fairing and saddlebag and doesn't crush your left leg, but the impact is enough to topple the bike over.

Perhaps the cars parked facing the arterial tricked you into thinking this was a one-way street. The narrow side street is actually two-way, which means a car could turn right from the arterial and come up the street. Even though you couldn't see a car about to turn, you could have predicted the possibility and stayed more to the right, to position yourself farther from a possible collision.

Signaling Slipups

Be sure you're giving the right signals for the situation.

You're on your way home from a ride in the country, gradually easing back into city traffic. You remember that great section of twisty roads that seemed to go on forever. But now you're almost home, and you are distracted by thoughts of the projects you need to finish before the weather turns.

You plan to make a right turn at the next intersection, so you thumb the turn-signal button as you move to the right lane and ease on the brake. You notice a white van in a condo parking lot, but it's not moving, and you're assuming it's parked.

But suddenly, the van pulls out, directly into your path. You're really startled because now you can see the van driver looking right at you. You attempt a quick stop, but it's too late. Your front wheel slams into the left side of the van. It's a slow-speed collision, and you're not injured, but the front wheel is bent, and of course you'll have to report the crash.

You're furious that the van driver pulled out right in front of you without warning. But then you realize that his view was partially blocked by a power pole. And even if he could have seen you, he could have misinterpreted your signal to mean that you were going to turn into the same driveway as he was exiting. It's possible he didn't see you or didn't realize you were signaling to turn into the side street a few feet further on.

Signaling your intention is always critical, but be sure you are giving clear signals for the situation. In this case, you could have signaled and changed lanes sooner, then cancelled your signals to separate the lane change from your intended turn. Then, after you passed the driveway with the van, you could have activated the right-turn signal again.

Because there was no way to know whether or not the van driver saw you, it would have been a wise precaution to slow or stop and wave him to proceed. It's important to control the situation, as well as your bike.

Slick Slowdowns

It's a good idea to take a break when it first starts to rain.

You're on your way home from a week-long trip, trying to make time on a busy freeway. The weather has been great until now, but suddenly the clouds roll in and it's pouring rain. You realize the surface will be slick, so you ride in the wheel tracks of vehicles ahead and make all control inputs smooth.

Suddenly, you realize a car is merging into your lane, just a few feet ahead of you, so you roll off the throttle. The driver doesn't accelerate, so you reach for the brake. The instant you squeeze on the brake to slow down, the front tire starts to slide, so you ease up. You're a little panicked because you are braking as hard as you dare and still you're closing in on the car ahead. Your front tire barely taps the bumper of the other car, and you both ease over to the shoulder to inspect the damage. There isn't even a mark on the car's bumper, and he doesn't want to stand around in the rain discussing it, so he just shrugs and drives away. You're thankful there was no damage and even more relieved that you didn't lose traction and fall down in freeway traffic.

Be aware that, during good weather, contaminants gradually build up on the surface of the pavement.

When it first starts to rain after a dry spell, the contaminants mix with water to form a very slippery goo. It takes about a half hour of steady rain to wash away the goo, during which time the roadway is extremely slick. It's very common for a surge in collisions to occur during a fresh rain.

In this situation, the car driver did you no favors by pulling in front of you without signaling and then not speeding up, but a motorcyclist must always be prepared to get out of the way. Rather than just continuing to ride in the suddenly slick conditions, the smarter tactic would have been to take a break for at least a half hour before continuing.

Slip Sliding

Steep uphill corners can be a problem.

For years, you've dreamed of making a trip to the West Coast to explore the winding roads along the coastline. And now you're finally making that dream come true, sharing the trip with a passenger. The secondary road you're following twists and turns, descends to the beach, and then suddenly climbs uphill around a tight right-hand switchback. You realize this is a really tight turn, so you slow way down and twist your head around to see if anyone is coming downhill.

But as you lean the bike sharply to the right, it loses speed trying to claw its way up the steep grade and threatens to lose balance. You roll on more throttle to regain control. But suddenly the front tire chirps sideways, and you have no option other than letting the bike drift wide into the downhill lane. Fortunately, there's no vehicle coming downhill, and you're able to recover and get back in your lane without dropping the bike, panicking your passenger, or causing a collision.

Remember that it's going to take energy to pull the bike and your load up a hill. And engine thrust is applied down at the contact patch of the rear tire, transferring weight off the front tire. The extra weight of a passenger and gear on the back of the bike also reduces front-tire traction—just where you need it to get the bike turned.

Enter an uphill corner at a slightly higher speed to provide more forward energy to carry the bike up and around. You can also enter the curve more from the outside to follow a path with a more consistent slope.

Slippery Bricks

Bricks are made of clay that gets slippery when wet.

You're exploring an old part of town, with lots of historic brick buildings, vintage street lights, and even some streets paved with bricks. It's enjoyable to explore on the bike because you can see so much more of the surroundings and even savor the scents, like the smell of the old pavement after a rain shower. You realize there are streetcar rails in the center of the one-way street, and you'd prefer to avoid crossing them, but a delivery truck has stopped in the right lane, blocking your way.

To get around the truck, you plan to cross over one rail to the brick area in the center, then swerve back to the right to cross the rail at a maximum angle. You're aware of how a rail can capture the front tire and cause a fall. But when you attempt to swerve back to the right to bounce over the rail, the front tire slides out on the bricks, and the bike slams onto its side. Apparently, the wet bricks were a lot more slippery than you would have expected.

Bricks are made of clay, and the tires of passing vehicles wear away the clay particles into a fine dust. When it rains, the clay dust mixes with water to create a slippery lubricant. Bricks can be a lot more slippery than they appear to be. The reduced traction affects both steering and braking. If at all possible, stay off wet bricks.

Had you been observing this situation more carefully, you might have realized that the truck is stopped for a red light, not a delivery. Attempting a pass at an intersection is not a good plan. You could simply have waited for the light to change and followed the truck through the intersection. You would have avoided both the rails and the brick surface and saved yourself a lot of grief.

Sloppy Slowdowns

Compression braking in the rain can dump you on your behind.

You've been out for a ride in the country, and now you're on the way home, approaching the outskirts of town. The weather was fine this morning when you left, but after lunch the black clouds moved in, and now it's a serious downpour. You always wear your armored all-weather riding gear, so you're well protected from the wet and cold. With the surface slippery, you ride a little slower and drop back a little farther behind the truck ahead to give yourself more maneuvering room.

The highway descends in a sweeping S turn, and you know the speed limit reduces to 35 mph. You decelerate as you normally would, shifting down as you blip the throttle, then rolling off to let compression braking slow the bike. At the bottom, you realize the signal light has turned red, so you ease on both brakes, favoring the rear pedal. But suddenly the rear tire loses traction, slides out, and dumps the bike on its low side. You're not injured, thanks to your riding gear, but it's a shock to lose control, and you know the bike has some embarrassing damage.

In this situation, the slippery downhill section required a more skillful braking technique to balance braking between both tires. You reverted to your "dry weather" habit of using only engine braking to slow down. Remember that engine-compression braking only applies to the rear wheel. And when riding downhill, more weight transfers from the rear wheel onto the front wheel, increasing front tire traction. A better technique for braking on a wet surface is to squeeze the clutch and apply both brakes smoothly and progressively.

Smokin' Stops

If you're sliding your tires, you're not stopping in the shortest distance.

You've made a stop at the post office to mail a letter, and now you're headed to the bike shop to talk about new tires. The weather isn't sunny and warm, but it's not raining, so the pavement is dry.

Suddenly, there's a beat-up camper van pulling out into your path. The gray-haired driver isn't even looking for other vehicles. You jam on the brakes to make a quick stop. As you squeeze on the front brakes, you hear the rear tire start to howl. You know a sliding rear tire isn't a big problem so long as you don't let up on the pedal, so you just keep it jammed on and let the tire smoke. Besides, if the tires are sliding aren't you making the quickest possible stop? Sure enough, you manage to stop short of a collision with the van. The driver just ignores you and keeps going.

A quick stop was the right evasive maneuver for this situation. But your situational awareness and braking techniques both need work. Although you noticed the beat-up condition of the camper—dirty, dented, and dinged up—you might have suspected that someone who doesn't care about her vehicle may also be a careless driver, unconcerned with other drivers on the road. The dents hint that this is not the first time this camper has headed toward a collision. Catching a glimpse of the driver's gray hair, you might also have assumed that the woman might be at an age when her mental processes have slowed—it happens! It would have been a wise precaution to brake sooner, to make more space for whatever this driver might have done.

When you do need to make a quick stop in the shortest distance, the best tactic is to brake just short of sliding the tires. Once a tire starts to slide, it loses traction. A smokin' stop might sound cool, but you can stop in a shorter distance if you don't slide the tires. One of the reasons riders opt for antilock (ABS) brakes is that they give riders confidence to brake aggressively without sliding the tires. Without ABS, however, you must brake smoothly and progressively on the front and ease up on the rear as weight transfers onto the front tire.

If you're riding a sport bike with a short wheelbase and powerful front brakes, it is also necessary to avoid braking so hard as to lift the rear wheel off the pavement. It is possible to do a forward loop on a lightweight bike.

Sport-bike Scrimmages

Drivers just don't give you any respect.

You really enjoy the performance of a superbike. You like the blazing acceleration, the heady speed, and the impressive cornering capabilities. You even admit to enjoying the scofflaw image that goes with a sport bike. However, you've noticed that drivers don't give you as much respect as the riders of most other machines. Some drivers will tailgate you, others will carelessly change lanes right in front of you. No one blames you for getting tired of seemingly blind drivers pulling out of side streets directly into your path at the last second. Why won't other motorists give sport-bike riders any respect?

Sport bikes are overrepresented in crashes and fatalities. Part of that may be that a high-performance machine encourages hooligan riding. When riding a fast and maneuverable bike, it's easy to take unnecessary risks, showing little respect for the laws or the safety of other motorists.

But consider that there are real reasons why a driver might pull out into the path of a fast-moving machine. Drivers expect that other vehicles will be moving at relatively the same speeds in traffic. If your superbike is approaching at a faster speed than surrounding traffic, a driver can easily misjudge your approach speed. It's a surprise to the driver who judges you to be moving at the speed of traffic to discover you arrive much more quickly than expected.

People often mistakenly judge distance based on size. A larger vehicle tends to appear closer, and a smaller vehicle appears to be farther away. So, where a full-dress cruiser may appear to be close, a narrow sport bike at the same distance may appear to be farther away.

To avoid the close calls resulting from predictable misjudgment of speed and distance, the rider of any small, narrow motorcycle must compensate. It helps to be conscious about positioning, both to separate yourself from other vehicles and to avoid being hidden from view. When in traffic on your sport bike, it's important that you maintain a speed similar to other vehicles and reduce speed aggressively when you observe a driver who might potentially misjudge your speed or distance.

Stale Signals

One clue to a stale green light is the pedestrian signal.

You've been commuting to work on the bike for the past year. At the moment, you're shuffling along a one-way arterial with numerous traffic signals. You'd prefer not to be caught running a red light, but neither do you want to be rear-ended if you stop too suddenly. The traffic lights on this street aren't synchronized, so it's hard to judge when a green light is about to turn amber.

Suddenly, your concerns become reality. Before you can clear an intersection, the green light turns amber, but the car ahead of you isn't moving. You're stranded in the intersection in the way of cross traffic. Drivers beep their horns in annoyance, and you're embarrassed to be caught in such a stupid situation. You're also a bit nervous about drivers attempting to turn and squeezing by inches away.

It's important to make a "go/no-go" decision before entering an intersection. If you can't see your way through, it's best to stop short. In most states, you can be ticketed for failing to clear the intersection, even if you are hemmed in by traffic. One good clue to a stale green light is the pedestrian signal. The pedestrian signal typically turns to "Don't walk" several seconds ahead of the vehicle signal to allow pedestrians to complete their crossing. If you can see that the pedestrian "Walk" light is still illuminated, it's a good bet that the green light will stay green for several more seconds. When it changes to "Don't walk," you should plan to stop before entering the intersection. Some pedestrian signals also have a visual countdown to show pedestrians how much time is left before it turns to "Don't walk."

Station Bumps

A little raised cover can be a rider's downfall.

Approaching the next exit, you can see two gas stations with easy access, and you pick one. But this isn't going to be an easy fill-up. Cars are blocking the pumps, and when you finally get the bike up to the pump, the credit card reader won't work. You walk in to pay a cash deposit, go back out to pump your gas, and go back inside to get your change from the surly attendant. All the delay is frustrating. Finally, you reset the bike's trip meter, zip up your jacket pockets, start the engine, and thread your way toward the street between the cars.

Suddenly, your front tire bounces sideways. You barely manage to maintain balance and not drop the bike. Looking down, you see a raised cover for an underground tank. The edges are steep and slippery. You're frustrated and anxious to be back out on the superslab again, and now you're furious about surface hazards that seem designed to cause trouble for a motorcyclist but not for a car driver.

Raised fill covers are a fact of life in gas stations today. They are just a bouncing nuisance for a car or truck, but if your front tire hits the angled edge, it can slide sideways. You're most likely to be surprised by such surface hazards when you're anxious or frustrated and not focusing on the entire situation.

When you find yourself in a frustrating situation, it's important to maintain your cool, so that you can be aware of even small hazards such as fill covers, drain grates, or slick surface markings while you're getting back on the road. You might consider pulling over to a corner of the lot and just chilling out or drinking a bottle of cool water.

Steely Slideouts

Steel construction plates can be a challenge.

You're heading out for a weekend ride early on a Saturday morning. Traffic is light at this hour and, once you get to the freeway, you can put down some miles and get out of town to your favorite back roads.

You're surprised to see a series of steel construction plates extending all the way across the right lane. They weren't there last weekend. You know steel can be very slippery, and there are several sharp edges that could hook your tires. So, you keep your tires in the right-wheel track to avoid most of the sharp edges and hold a steady throttle to minimize tire slip.

But just before the bike bumps over the steel, you realize the traffic light ahead has turned red. Out of habit, you ease off the throttle and apply the brakes. The rear tire slides left on the shiny steel, then snaps right as the tire bounces off the steel and hooks up on the asphalt. It's a close call, and you're really surprised at the rear end stepping out.

You were smart to avoid the sharp edges of the steel plates, and your technique to hold a steady throttle while in a curve was spot on. But, in this situation, it would have been better to ride straight across the steel with the bike upright. You had adequate space to ride a straight line and to stay off the brakes until the tires were off the steel. Most importantly, you should not have allowed yourself to be so focused on the surface hazard that you weren't observing the rest of the situation, including the traffic signal ahead.

Steep Stops

Whatever you find difficult— that's what you need to practice.

You've always been a bit paranoid about stopping on steep hills. You'd prefer to put both feet on the ground, but the front brake can't seem to keep the bike from rolling back downhill, and it's hard to operate the front brake and throttle simultaneously as you attempt to get it moving.

At the moment, you're starting to sweat because you're climbing a steep hill, and there's a Stop sign at the top. To make matters worse, it's an odd junction with a small roundabout in the center and four Stop signs. You're hoping you can just ease up to the Stop sign and, if no one is coming, you'll keep rolling and make your left turn. You'll be fine as long as no other vehicles happen along.

Then, just as you reach the Stop sign, a car suddenly appears on your right. But you're committed to continue your turn without stopping, and besides, the driver needs to stop. But as you ease into the intersection, the car blows through the Stop sign and accelerates into your path. To avoid a collision, you jam on the brakes, but, with the bike leaned over, you're not prepared to hold it up. It crashes over on its left side as the other driver roars off.

You're furious that the other driver failed to stop for the sign, but, of course, you also should have come to a complete stop before proceeding. In any case, your bike is scratched and dented, as is your ego. You're ashamed that your deficient skills persuaded you to ignore the law.

Always bring the bike to a stop with both brakes and in first gear. Your left foot should always support the bike at a stop, so that your right foot can be on the rear brake. To get started heading uphill, it will be necessary to rev the engine more than usual and to slip the clutch. As the bike begins to pull uphill, release the brakes. With practice, you will learn to roll on enough throttle to get the bike moving without stalling the engine.

Either your skills are declining, or you're improving them by practice. Whatever you find difficult—that's what you need to practice. If stopping and starting on hills is your recurring nightmare, the fix is to practice stopping and starting on hills. If practicing on your heavyweight roadburner is an issue, borrow a smaller bike for your initial practice.

Stone Salvos

It's a good idea to stay far away from big dump trucks.

You're heading home on the bike, fighting your way through afternoon traffic. You maintain plenty of following distance behind the vehicles ahead and watch carefully for drivers who might suddenly change lanes. The gravel truck on your left appears to be staying in the lane, but you're nervous about such a big and noisy vehicle so close. You know that the view in a truck driver's mirrors is limited. You're wondering if you should drop back or ease over to the right side of your lane.

Then, traffic begins to move, and as the truck starts to get the load moving, a large stone shoots out from the truck's drive wheels. You duck, but the rock nails your helmet, right above the face shield. Apparently, a stone from the gravel pit had been trapped between two tires. You're stunned but not injured. Later, you'll learn that your helmet shell is cracked.

Trucks that haul loose material such as gravel, dirt, sawdust, or scrap steel are likely to spit dangerous objects onto the road. A loose stone or piece of wood may be riding on the frame or temporarily caught between two tires. Even at urban speeds, a thrown

object such as a stone can crack a car's windshield—
but for a motorcyclist, it can be deadly. When you
observe a truck such as this gravel hauler, it's smart to
move away from it.

In this situation, there wasn't a lot you could have
done to avoid an unseen hazard, which is why
experienced riders always wear protective gear. A
cracked helmet is an expensive loss, but not as costly
or potentially life-changing as a head injury.

Subject to Flooding

Just because it's not raining doesn't mean the road ahead isn't under water.

For years, you've wanted to explore some of the desert country in the Southwest, and you're finally here, dawdling along old Route 66 between California and Arizona. The summer weather is hot and dry, and everything is a burnt brown color. The historic road is bumpy and patched, but it's enjoyable on your street machine. It's peaceful and quiet out here. You're a little startled to come upon a Subject to Flooding sign way out in the desert, miles from the nearest river. It must be a joke for the tourists, you think.

But as you round the next corner and approach a dip in the road, you're startled to see a torrent of dirty water rushing across the road and roaring off toward the horizon. You stop and wonder whether your bike could make it across. The water is only about 30 feet wide, but you're not sure how deep it is or whether the pavement is still there. What impresses you is the speed of the rushing water. You decide to turn around and go back to a hotel in the last town for the night.

You mention the flooded wash to a casino patron and get an earful about flash floods in the desert. A thunderstorm miles away can suddenly drop a torrent of rain, which rushes across the dry landscape, picking up speed and debris. The flash flood can travel for miles, tearing out roads in its path. Motorists who foolishly attempt to cross a flooded wash are typically swept away. Just a foot of water moving at 30 mph is enough to push a heavy truck off the road. The locals guffaw at your thoughts of attempting to cross the flooded wash on your motorcycle. They suggest you look for the old campfire circles on the hills near a wash, where people would camp for days, waiting for the water to go down.

It's good that your common sense won out over your adventurous side. It's very unlikely you would have made it across.

Surviving Dumb Stunts

You need to be prepared for all sorts of dumb driving.

You're enjoying a pleasant ride in the mountains. Traffic is light, the weather is warm and sunny, and the pavement is clean and dry. The curvy road invites you to enjoy it at a good clip.

Suddenly, rounding a blind left-hander, you realize there's a motor home blocking both lanes. You immediately transition to the brakes and barely manage a stop just short of a collision. The driver just shrugs at you and takes off. You were fortunate that it wasn't a blind right-hand turn, where your sight distance would have been much shorter. You can't believe anyone would try a dumb stunt like that.

Sometimes it's hard to comprehend the asinine, improbable maneuvers other drivers will attempt. Apparently, this guy needed to make a U-turn and didn't see any problem with attempting it in the middle of a highway. Unfamiliar with how much room his rental vehicle would take to U-turn, he had to do some backing and filling.

To survive such dumb stunts, you need to keep your head in the ride and think way ahead of your machine. It's not that you can or should predict some nimrod like this blocking the road around every blind corner. More to the point, when you are rounding any corner where your sight distance is limited, think about what hazards might be hidden from view. Before you're too close, you can begin transitioning to braking while you still have time.

When you are surprised by some hazard, your evasive action will be determined by your habits. So, when cornering on a road with limited views, it's a good habit to transition from throttle to brake, to build the muscle memory to brake automatically when needed. And, of course, it will help if you periodically practice quick stops away from traffic.

Suspension Subversion

Sacked suspension isn't just a matter of less comfort.

You really enjoy riding your bike in the country. There's less traffic, cleaner air, and often a more pleasant view. You've owned this same bike for a number of years, and, in fact, it has a lot of its original parts. You do buy high-quality tires because you're aware that tires are very important for good traction. The ride is a little bumpy, but not too bad, so you haven't been eager to spend big bucks on suspension upgrades. One of these days, you plan to check your shock preload, but the damping is beyond your talents.

Like most secondary roads, this one gets little maintenance, so you're careful to skirt potholes and pick the smoothest pavement. But suddenly, as you are leaning into a right-hand sweeper, the wheels begin to chatter and bounce. The well-worn suspension on your old bike just can't absorb the bumps and ripples, and the tires are actually bouncing off the pavement. You dab on the brakes, but that only makes matters worse. You let the bike drift wide across the centerline as you get it slowed. Luckily, there's no oncoming traffic at the moment. You avoid a crash, but now you're fully aware of how a sacked suspension is more than just a comfort consideration.

Obviously, you understand the need to periodically buy new tires. As with tires, shocks and springs also need periodic upgrades. It's not realistic to expect that the original suspension will continue to work just as it came from the factory for years and years. Even with a new bike, it's important to set up your suspension for the weight you'll be carrying, so that both front and rear not only support the load in the middle of shock travel but also help keep the tires in contact with the pavement when rolling over bumps and dips. Original suspension typically starts to fade by about 30,000 miles even if it's set up properly. For your old bike, it's obviously time for a suspension upgrade, which will be cheaper than a crash.

Taillight Fixation

It's easy to get sucked into trouble when you're in fast company.

Lately, you've been socializing with some riders who ride machines similar to yours, and you've been invited to go along with them on a group ride. You're a little surprised by the aggressiveness of the other riders, who seem to want to turn every ride into a race. You realize you may be in a bit over your head with these guys, but your ego is at stake, so you attempt to hang with them in close formation.

Suddenly, in a tight left-hand turn, your bike drifts a little too wide. You panic and snap the throttle closed, and the bike crashes. You're not seriously injured, except for your ego. The other riders don't even stop to help.

Group rides can be a real blast, but the social pressure of trying to keep up with other riders can get you into trouble, and different groups have different attitudes about managing the dangers. Different riders also have different levels of skill and knowledge, and you should never assume you can hang with a group of riders you don't know.

Well-organized group rides can be a lot of fun, but some states have reported a significant increase in fatalities occurring on group rides. One big factor is the social pressure of trying to keep up with the group, some of whom may be more willing than you are to take unnecessary chances.

It's tempting to just fixate on the taillight of the bike ahead and ride as fast as you can. To avoid being caught in a situation where you're in over your head, it's important to ride your own ride. That is, drop back far enough behind the rider ahead so that you have to make your own decisions about speed, cornering lines, and surface hazards. A good ride leader will allow that to happen.

But if the other riders attempt to make you feel inferior about your riding, perhaps that's a signal that you need to drop out of this ride and find a different group.

Tar Snakes

That crack sealer may be a lot more slippery than you might think.

You're out for a Sunday ride, following a state highway you know will provide both fun corners and great scenery. This is a favorite ride, and you have a pretty good idea of the twists and turns, so you can ride a bit aggressively. You notice numerous areas where a maintenance crew apparently applied crack sealer. You're not overly concerned since the sealer seems to have been applied smoothly.

But suddenly, as you lean the bike over into a left-hand sweeper, you feel your rear tire twitch. It's enough of an unexpected surprise that you panic a bit and roll off the throttle. That seems to make matters worse. The rear end steps out, and the bike drops onto its left side and slides off onto the shoulder. You're not injured, although your riding gear is scuffed, and the bike now has some serious scratches and a couple of new dents. As you get the bike upright, you're angry that the road crew would put down this slippery sealer without warning signs.

Different maintenance departments use different crack sealer compounds and different application techniques. The cheapest sealer has about half the friction of asphalt pavement. Some states use crack sealer that contains abrasives and then apply further abrasives to the surface.

When you observe "tar snakes," it would be smart to choose cornering lines that avoid the slick sealer as much as possible. If you can't avoid the tar snakes, reduce speed to reduce traction demands.

Target Fixation

The bike tends to go where you're looking.

You're riding an urban arterial and stop for a red light. There's a steel construction plate sticking out partially into your lane, and the sharp edge makes you nervous. You focus on the plate as you ease

out the clutch. But you're shocked when the bike steers itself directly toward the edge and catches the front tire. Suddenly, you lose balance, and the bike goes down.

You're the victim of "target fixation," the tendency to subconsciously steer a vehicle toward an object that you're focusing on. You were staring at the edge of the steel plate, and that's where you inadvertently pointed the bike.

When you observe hazards such as a pothole or edge trap, it's essential to avoid staring directly at it; instead, you must focus on a path around the problem. For instance, in this situation, you could have focused on the clear pavement to the left of the steel plate, which would have helped steer the bike around it.

Tentative Turners

If a driver appears to be confused, stay out of the way.

You're riding a familiar urban arterial, approaching a shopping center. There is a left-turn lane on the left, divided from the other lanes by white lines. You've noticed the car ahead has an out-of-state plate, and the driver changes speed erratically. You suspect the driver might be confused and undecided about where to turn. You're relieved when the driver enters the left-turn lane. You can get back up to speed.

But just as you are passing the car, the driver suddenly swerves back across the line into your path. You squeeze over to a lane-splitting position to avoid a collision and then accelerate to get out of the way. It was a close call, and you can barely control your rage at the driver's stupid maneuver. He apparently didn't see you or was so flustered by the situation that he just swerved without looking.

You did the right thing by getting out of his way. Even though you had the right-of-way, that's little consolation when you're lying on the pavement after a collision.

It's not enough to be in control of your bike: you need to be in control of the situation in which you are riding. If you just wait to react to what happens, you'll need to be very quick. So, rather than just react, learn to predict what's going to happen so that you can take evasive action earlier. In this situation, you did see some hints that the driver was unfamiliar with the traffic pattern. You could have predicted he might do something strange. You could have accelerated or dropped back earlier to allow for the driver to change his mind.

Tight-line Terror

Maybe it's not too smart following a racing line on a public road.

You're riding in a part of the state where you haven't been before, and you're pleased that the road you're on is turning out to be great—lots of twists and turns, smooth pavement, and very little traffic. You took a track school several months ago, where the instructor promoted hanging off and following a "tight" cornering line. You're trying that out now, maintaining an aggressive speed, shifting weight to the inside of the saddle, and staying close to the white fog line as you round a sweeping right-hander. You're imagining that you're on a racetrack in the forest.

But just as you pass the apex, you realize there's a car stopped in the road ahead so someone can snap a picture. You manage to control your reactions, pushing hard on the left grip to lift the bike up and swerve around the car, then pushing hard on the right grip to lean back into your lane, and pushing hard on the left grip to straighten up. You make it, but you're shocked at how quickly the ride went from fun to terror. If another vehicle had been in the opposite lane, there wouldn't have been anywhere to go to escape a crash. You're instantly angry at the stupidity of some tourists to stop in the road halfway around a blind curve.

Give yourself a pat on the back for pulling off a successful quick swerve, but then think about the important lesson here: it's not smart to try transferring your track techniques to public roads. Unlike the track, there are lots of hazards on public roads, including wild animals, fallen trees, rock slides, and, yes, cars stopped in inappropriate places. Riding aggressively on public roads jacks up the risks, especially where the view ahead is limited. Rather than blaming the driver for doing something that put you at risk, you might use this close call as an opportunity to rethink your riding tactics.

If you wish to avoid collisions, you must always be able to bring the bike to a complete stop within your sight distance, which means not only braking when the vanishing point retracts but also positioning the bike for the best view ahead. If you had moved closer to the centerline before turning the bike in, you would have had a much better view through the turn and very likely could have seen the car sooner.

Tire Failures

Last week's low tire pressure can turn into this week's blowout.

You're three days and two thousand miles from home. Your bike has been carrying a huge load of gear, including some tools and spares. You're constantly amazed at how well the bike handles at a good speed and seldom needs any maintenance. You just gas it up and go.

You sense you had a little problem the first day out, when you felt the rear end wiggling around. At first, you thought it was just a result of the extra load, but after several hours, the wiggling seemed worse, so you pulled off at a rest area to see what was going on. You discovered that the rubber valve stem had cracked, and the tire was almost flat. You rode slowly to the next town, where a motorcycle shop replaced the valve stem and pumped the tire back up to pressure. The tire appeared to be in excellent condition.

Now, two days later and only a half hour into the ride, you feel the rear dancing around again. You stop at the next rest area to check it out. You're shocked to find that the tire is completely deflated, the tread blocks are partially melted, and there's a spot where the belts have let go. You're angered at the tire failure, and promise yourself to never buy *that* brand again.

Before you blame the tire (or the manufacturer), remember that you had ridden for days, possibly weeks, on a low tire. Pumping it back up to pressure after solving the leak couldn't undo the damage. It wasn't your choice of a tire brand that caused the eventual failure, but your lack of attention to tire pressure. Today's steel-belted motorcycle tires are so stiff that a deflated tire may not look low on pressure or even feel flat on the road. But a low tire will flex enough at highway speed to generate destructive heat that permanently damages the rubber and weakens the fabric cords. It's not a bad idea to check tire pressures every morning during a long ride. Many riders carry a small electric pump to make it easier to maintain tire pressures while traveling.

Tire Sliders

How can a smashed can cause so much trouble?

You're headed out for a ride with some friends. You look forward to riding with people you can trust, and you're all hyped up about the quick trip up the canyon to the biker hangout. After breakfast, everyone suits up and gets ready to roll.

As the group leaves the parking lot, you observe a tin can mashed flat by other vehicles. You decide to mash it even flatter by riding over it on your way out. But, just as your front tire rolls over the can, the rider ahead of you brakes to let a car go by. You squeeze the front brake lever, but for some reason your bike won't stop. You squeeze harder, but your front wheel just slides ahead, right into the other bike.

You're embarrassed to hit the other rider and even more embarrassed to crash during a group ride where all your buddies will hear about it. The truth is that you can't blame your front brake. When you braked, the front tire grabbed the flattened can, and the can slid across the pavement like a ski. There wasn't anything wrong with your front brake, only your judgment.

When you're out riding with a group, it's common to be "feeling your oats" and looking for some way to show off. It might seem cool to kick your boot through a pile of leaves as you ride away, pull off a "stoppie" with your rear tire in the air, or mash a can flat. But it's best to control such urges. The pile of leaves may be hiding some slick mud or ball-bearing-like acorns. The pavement may have a streak of diesel oil or sand right where you intend to brake. And a flat object such as a tin can or ice cream carton can turn into an embarrassing "tire slider." The truly clever rider keeps the stunts in check and avoids any unnecessary embarrassment.

Touchdown Trouble

When your bike touches down in the corners, is it the machine or is it your technique?

You don't mind cruising the freeways on your powerful machine, but you really prefer the secondary highways, especially those with lots of technical turns and elevation changes. Today, you're riding with some other motorcyclists who seem to prefer an aggressive pace, and you attempt to keep up, lest they think you aren't as skilled a rider.

Although you're riding the same bike as two of the others, yours seems to touch down more at the fast pace. You're concerned that touching down the sidestand or exhaust pipes might lever the bike off the tires and cause a crash. To keep up with the others, you accelerate hard in the straights and brake as you lean into the turns. As you enter a tight left-hander, the bike squats into a dip, and you feel something touch down hard. You immediately lift the bike up, roll off, and brake, but that just points the machine into the roadside fence. You're not injured much in the crash, but it's very embarrassing losing control while attempting to keep up.

Part of the problem may be your machine. Touching down is a sign of a suspension problem. Take the effort to get your suspension set properly for your weight and the load you carry. Check your tire pressures before you head out on an aggressive ride, and inspect the tire treads to ensure you'll have adequate traction. Avoid making any modifications to the machine that will reduce leanover clearance.

You might also consider your cornering tactics. A cornering line with a greater radius requires less lean angle for the same speed. Easing on some throttle after the turn-in will help keep the bike up on the suspension. That may require that you brake to a slower speed before you lean the bike and then sneak on the throttle as you lean. Shifting your weight toward the inside of the curve will allow the bike to corner at less of an angle. Learn to transition smoothly between brakes and throttle to avoid any sudden inputs.

Transient Traction

Does that change in the color of the pavement mean a change in traction?

It's been a good day for exploring the country. The bike has been running great, the weather is just right, and you remember the road from previous rides. You're not in a hurry today, so you just putter along, enjoying the scenery and thinking about tasks waiting at home. You notice a change in the color of the pavement ahead continuing through the corner, but it doesn't cause you any special concern.

But, just as soon as your tires run onto the different surface, you feel the front tire start to slide around, and you realize there is loose gravel spread onto fresh tar. The bike feels as if it's going to slide out and fall down, so you roll off the throttle and lean the bike as gently as possible toward the left. But it feels so unsteady that you let the bike drift wider toward the shoulder.

Suddenly, your tires plow into the deeper gravel near the guardrail, and the bike goes down. It's a slow-speed crash, and you're not seriously injured. One turn signal is broken, and the sidecovers are scratched. And now you're really concerned about any other patched areas along this road.

It's important to constantly maintain your awareness of the situation, including the road surface. You might have observed the gravel berm along the centerline, where passing vehicles have thrown it. And you could have seen that the white line disappeared under the repaired surface. When riding on loose gravel with street tires, it helps to keep the bike more vertical and to steer with the throttle—that is, use short bursts of throttle to slide the rear end out and point the bike where you want it to go. To prepare yourself for such situations, it would help to borrow a dirt bike and get in some practice on loose or slippery surfaces.

Trashy Trucks

Some commercial trucks trail a steady stream of debris.

You've found the time to make a cross-country trip and, at the moment, you're crossing Wyoming on the freeway. You notice a lot of truck traffic, big dump trucks carrying some sort of loose material. You assume there must be a mine nearby. The drivers seem to be reasonably courteous, so you just cruise on by in the left lane.

But where the freeway curves around a hill, you suddenly find yourself downwind, and the loose material is blowing out right into your path. You're shocked at the gritty material suddenly spraying at your paint and windshield, and some even finds its way into your eyes. Even though you can't see well, you roll on the throttle to pull ahead and get out of the abrasive grit. You're angry at a trucking firm that would allow open trucks on the freeway, but you realize that there is nothing you can do other than get out of the way.

Commercial trucks do carry loose material that blows out in the wind. In addition to dinging your paint and plastic, grit in your eyes can cause you to lose control. What's more, loose material on the road surface can reduce traction. You're correct that there is nothing you can do. Commercial interests will always trump the complaints of a passing motorcyclist.

When you observed the open dump trailer, you should have predicted there would be material blowing out and planned to pass the truck when it was downwind of you. You can also expect debris to be kicked up by any large boxes, such as trailers and RVs. The turbulent air swirling around a big box picks up dirt and sand from the shoulder and spreads it into the slipstream. It's best to avoid being passed by such vehicles. If you can't avoid being passed, drop back quickly to escape the storm of debris.

Tricky Tracks

Streetcar tracks require a clever plan of attack.

Since this morning's weather is nice, you decide to ride the bike rather than drive the car to your business meeting. Parking will be easier, and frankly, you want to impress the others with your adventurous spirit.

As you approach the downtown area, you remember that there are streetcar tracks. You hadn't really been bothered by the rails when driving your car, but now you realize that the paving between the rails is uneven, and there are lots of slots and grooves. You find yourself between two rails that are heading for the wrong side of the street, and so you attempt to lean the bike and ease over the rails to get back toward the right. Suddenly, your front tire is captured by the slot alongside a rail, and it slides. You struggle to keep the bike balanced, but the tire goes one way and the bike topples the other way. You eventually get to the meeting, but your freshly scratched helmet and scuffed gear are a giveaway that you've just experienced the dangerous side of motorcycling—not exactly the dashing image you had intended.

Remember that two-wheelers are balanced primarily by steering the front wheel to keep the tire contact points balanced under the center of mass. If you can't steer, you can't balance. When your front tire rolls up to a rail or slot at a narrow angle, it tends to slide along the rail rather than roll across. To avoid falling when crossing shiny rails, steer away from the rail, then swerve back and attack the rail at a maximum angle, preferably 45 degrees or greater. The greater the attack angle, the less likely that the rail, or a slot alongside the rail, will capture your tire. It's especially important to keep your tires away from any "V" or "X" connections where rails join or cross.

U-turn Technique

Making tight U-turns can be tricky, but practice will help.

You're looking for a place to park for the breakfast meeting. The crowd of riders on the sidewalk turns to look as you motor by. All of the easy spaces are—unfortunately for you—already taken, and the street comes to an end. You need to make a tight U-turn to avoid hitting any of the parked bikes. And frankly, you've always had trouble with U-turns.

If it weren't for the riders watching, you would just paddle walk the bike back and forth to get it turned around. But that would peg you as a novice. So, you just swing wide, turn the bike as tight as it will go, and hope it will idle around in a half circle. Unfortunately, the bike goes a little wide and, to avoid hitting the parked machines, you grab the clutch. The bike immediately crashes over on its side. Onlookers come over to help lift the bike up, but your pride is mortally wounded.

The key to making a tight turn is leaning the bike way over. The greater the lean angle, the tighter the turn radius. That requires you to counterlean, shifting more of your weight to the outside footpeg. To prevent the bike from falling over, it's important to keep the engine pulling, so ease on a bit of throttle and slip the clutch as needed. Look where you want to go, not at the ground in front of the bike. If you have independent brakes, it may help to drag the rear brake to give the engine something to pull against.

If you find U-turns difficult, the way to make them easier is to practice. Set up some cones to make a box with an open end, about 20 feet square. As you gain skill, pull the sides in. Eventually, you should be able to do a U-turn within 14 feet—less than the width of a narrow street.

View Blockers

Hiding behind big vehicles can lead to surprises.

You're riding a nice country road, eager to enjoy the curves at a more invigorating speed. Traffic is light but, at the moment, there is a concrete truck holding you up. You move up close behind the truck, planning to make a quick pass if the opposing lane is clear.

As you follow the truck around a curve, you move over to look ahead. There's an oncoming car, so you duck back in behind the truck, expecting to take another look after the car passes. Suddenly, the car is making a left turn behind the truck, and there's nothing you can do to prevent a collision. Your front wheel slams into the car's passenger door, the forks fold back under the engine, and you are catapulted over the top. You slam into the pavement and slide down the road a few feet, and fortunately you don't slide into a tree or a power pole.

The ride is over for today, and probably for the rest of the year. At the ER, you are informed that your riding gear protected you from abrasions, but you have a fractured collar bone and three broken ribs. You survived the crash, but you can't help turning it over and over in your mind, wondering what you could have done to avoid it.

You might have been thinking of the truck as just a hindrance to your progress, but the most important concept is that big vehicles block the view, especially if you are close. It's not just a matter of not being able to see ahead of the truck—oncoming drivers will not be able to see you. From the perspective of the driver, there was just a space behind the truck, with plenty of room to make a left turn into a driveway.

It's never smart to follow close behind big, view-blocking vehicles such as trucks or busses. If possible, avoid riding behind them at all times. But if you must follow a big vehicle, drop back to open up the view so you can see more of what's coming and other drivers can see you.

Windy Wambles

What do you do when a gust of wind pushes you toward the centerline?

You've been itching for a long ride ever since the weather started warming up, and this weekend you decide that motorcycling will take top priority. The weather isn't likely to be very warm, but at least there's no rain in the forecast. Friday night, you tend the engine oil and tire pressures, lubricate cable ends, snug up all the fasteners, stow your electric vest, and wipe the bike clean. Saturday morning, you suit up and roll the bike out.

Leaving town, you try to recall all the survival tactics, such as staying out of the blind spots of trucks,

watching for left-turning vehicles at intersections, and avoiding loose sand berms left from wintertime maintenance. You intend to have a long, hard ride, not spend the day filling out accident forms.

After lunch, you find the winds have picked up, with occasional nasty gusts. As you're halfway across a bridge, suddenly a strong gust blasts you from the right, pushing the bike toward the oncoming trucks. You almost sideswipe a dump truck before the gust abates, and you're able to get the bike back onto your side of the road. The gust surprised you, and you're shocked that you couldn't keep the bike from being blown into oncoming traffic.

To counter a wind gust, you need to get the bike leaned upwind as quickly as possible. The only way to get the bike leaned quickly is to steer the front wheel. To counter a gust from your right, you must press both grips toward the right to get the bike leaned over into the wind. Then, when the gust abates, you'll need to press the grips toward the left to roll the bike vertical again. You can often see clues about wind gusts from foliage or surrounding water, and you should always expect crosswinds when you're riding over a bridge.

Wobbly Turns

Maybe your bike has a problem—or maybe your skills need work.

When you got into motorcycling a couple of years ago, you bought a used bike, a big V-twin. At first, when you were just learning how to ride, you took it easy, especially on curvy roads. But now that you've gained some experience and confidence, you're beginning to corner a bit faster, and you're starting to notice that the bike handles strangely.

The bike tends to wobble and weave in turns. Sometimes the wobble is so unnerving that you allow it to drift wider rather than risk a crash. It's like the bike can't decide whether to straighten up or keep turning. You're wondering if there is something wrong with the machine. It's good to pay attention to any strange handling, as this could be a clue to a real problem. Maybe your steering head bearings need servicing, or your front fork oil needs topping up. Maybe your old shock absorbers are ready for replacement. A motorcyclist needs to pay constant attention to maintenance issues, including suspension setup and tire pressures.

Or, maybe it's your cornering technique. The bike will be steadier if you decelerate in a straight line before entering a curve and then transition from brakes to throttle as you lean in. Remember that a bike is leaned by momentarily pressing the grips toward the direction that you want to go. For example, to lean the bike toward the right, momentarily press the grips toward the right. You can't steer the bike into a turn without first getting it leaned over.

The cornering lines you follow are also important. Rather than just following a "car" line in the center of the lane, follow an "outside-inside-outside" line. For instance, initiate a right turn from closer to the centerline. Start a left turn from closer to the right-side fog line. That allows a cornering line with a greater radius than the pavement, resulting in less of a lean angle for the same speed.

Wood-plank Perils

Wood surfaces can be surprisingly slick when wet.

Despite a few rain showers, today's ride has been great. You've been following an old highway that curves through farmland, crossing a few creeks and gullies here and there. You're in no hurry, but you maintain a somewhat aggressive pace to fully enjoy the bike.

You know that on secondary roads such as this the pavement isn't always well maintained, so you try to put your tires over the most tractable surface, while avoiding the potholes and ripples. And where the road passes near farms, you ride more conservatively when you see mud, manure, and hay tracked onto the surface.

You really appreciate that this road is so little used that it's never been a priority to straighten it out and widen it. Many of the bridges are the originals, with rumbly wooden decks, and the bridge ahead is in a curve. You lean the bike in and prepare to feel the rumble-rumble as your tires pound over the thick, uneven planks.

It's a bit of a shock when your tires slip sideways on the planks. You hold a steady throttle and let the bike drift a little wider. The tires regain traction, but the side slip certainly got your attention. The wood planks certainly looked uneven but not slick.

Wood fibers get ground away from the planks by the tires of passing vehicles. When dry, traction can be very acceptable. But when wet, the wood fibers mix with water to form a very slippery paste. This bridge was still damp from the earlier rain showers and now is very slippery, which wouldn't have been as much of a problem if the bridge wasn't curved.

In this situation, you could have better maintained traction by planning a straighter line across the bridge to keep the bike more vertical and reduce the side loads.

A bridge like this is most slippery after a brief shower or when wet with morning dew. Heavy rain will wash away much of the accumulated wood fiber and provide better traction.

Index

About the Author

David L. Hough (pronounced "huff") is a longtime motorcyclist, motorcycle journalist, and safety instructor with more than forty-eight years and a million miles of experience. Dave and his wife Diana live near Port Angeles, Washington, about 80 miles northwest of Seattle. They have traveled extensively by motorcycle on several different continents, visiting places across the United States, Canada, Brazil, central Europe, Great Britain, Ireland, South Africa, and New Zealand.

Dave was employed by The Boeing Company in Seattle for more than thirty-six years, and much of that time he commuted to work daily by motorcycle. His commuting and travel experiences provided an ongoing stream of ideas that led to articles on riding skills. He contributed to a number of motorcycle magazines over the years, including the "Proficient Motorcycling" and "Street Strategies" columns in *Motorcycle Consumer News* and the "Between the Ears" column in *BMW Owners News*. He currently contributes to *Iron Butt Magazine* and *BMW Motorcycle Magazine* and generates online columns for www.SoundRider.com.

Over the years Dave has written several books, including *Proficient Motorcycling*, *Street Strategies*, *Mastering the Ride*, *Driving a Sidecar Outfit*, and *The Good Rider*. He is an accomplished illustrator, photographer, lecturer, carpenter, fabricator, mechanic, and gardener; one of the few motorcycle journalists in the world who has also been a certified motorcycle safety instructor.

Dave has taught both two-wheeled and three-wheeled-motorcycle training courses. Many of his ideas on rider training have been absorbed into courses developed by the Motorcycle Safety Foundation. He wrote the sidecar course that became the basis for the Sidecar/Trike Education Program currently offered at training sites across the nation. He continues to offer riding skills seminars at various motorcycle events. At seventy-six years of age, Dave still rides, but he is down to one motorcycle.

Hough has received awards for his writing, including special commendations from the Motorcycle Safety Foundation and the BMWMOA Foundation. In recognition of his lifetime efforts toward motorcycle safety, he was inducted into the AMA Motorcycle Hall of Fame in 2009.